the Gluten-Free Grains

cookbook

75 Wholesome Recipes Worth Sharing

Featuring Buckwheat, Millet, Sorghum, Teff, Wild Rice and More

RECIPES AND FOOD STYLING BY
Quelcy Kogel
Founder of With the Grains

PHOTOGRAPHY BY
Noah Purdy

PAGE STREET
PUBLISHING CO.

PAGE STREET
PUBLISHING CO.

Copyright © 2019 by Quelcy Kogel

First published in 2019 by
Page Street Publishing Co.
27 Congress Street, Suite 105
Salem, MA 01970
www.pagestreetpublishing.com

Distributed by Macmillan, sales in Canada by The Canadian Manda Group.

23   22   21   20   19   1   2   3   4   5

ISBN-13: 978-1-62414-698-5
ISBN-10: 1-62414-698-8

Library of Congress Control Number: 2018960452

Cover and book design by Rosie Stewart for Page Street Publishing Co.
Photography by Noah Purdy
Food styling by Quelcy Kogel

Printed and bound in China

To Regina. You always shared more than you had.
You gave everything, so I could explore the wildest of
paths. This book would not exist if not for you.

And to you, dear reader. I'm so grateful you're here.
Now, more than ever, we need to come together.

Contents

Sunday Suppers
Slow Down & Enjoy the Process

Lite Bites & Appetizers
Gussied Up Grains

Soups & Stews
Creamy Grains

Sides & Salads
A Grainy Crunch

Dessert
Don't Go to Bed Salty

Welcome to My Table

Hello, dear reader, and welcome. I'm Quelcy (like "Quell the sea"), and this is an invitation for you to join me. I've saved you a seat, and I'd like to offer you a cheese board and a glass of wine while we talk through purple lips about our cliché love of all things French. Let's pack an epic picnic lunch to enjoy at the flea market. Let's toast champagne on Sunday mornings and refill our coffee cups *at least* once. And let's end with something sweet. I *always* want to end with something sweet. But before we end, let's get started.

My relationship with food has not always been harmonious. I once deprived myself as much as I could. I relished the false sense of control starvation can bring, but physical emptiness also brings loneliness and heartache. Over time, I began to heal myself, slowly. I began to reconnect, and eventually, I came to relish the way food not only nourishes the body, but fills the heart and soul if grown and prepared in earnest.

I began to wander cities and countries, wrapping my brain and mouth around different languages, traditions and foods. I learned to enjoy and respect food, *real* food. In doing so, I found a new appreciation for the generations of farmers who preceded me, the men and women who worked the land and were always ready with a meal for someone in need. The more I learned, the more lessons I realized I had squandered. The daughter of a cattleman and a descendent of farmers, I wanted to restore my agricultural roots in an effort to restore my own connection to food.

I found myself baking and cooking, at first simply to avoid the ingredients I didn't trust. However, in these kitchen experiments, I found a new communion. I found the same creative fulfillment I once found through pencil lines on sketchbook pages. A nostalgic at heart, I picked up a camera to collect these recipes like postcards, preserving places and times, and shared them on my own corner of the web, WithTheGrains.com.

Grains became my emblem, but my interest in grains has always been rooted in agriculture, in the men and women who stick to their values, who use nature's genius instead of man's chemicals. Fittingly, I fell in love with Kyle, an organic farmer and beekeeper, who I have dubbed "The Rustbelt Farmer." Life has a way of coming full circle.

Kyle's harvests inspire me. I love to cook and bake for others, to invite friends and *their* friends to join us in our dining room, and I always volunteer to bring a dessert to family functions. What I don't love is watching someone feel excluded because he or she can't eat the dessert everyone else is enjoying. Gluten allergies and sensitivities have been on the rise, so whether you have to avoid gluten, love someone who does or just want to host a more inclusive gathering, I created these recipes with sharing in mind.

The other motivating factor for this book was health. There are now many gluten-free products on the market daily (even my shampoo is gluten-free), and the marketing buzz wants us to believe these items are healthier. However, when you take the time to read these labels, the product is often filled with preservatives, starches and binders that can be just as difficult to digest as gluten or are the nutritional equivalent of white bread.

I in no way want to mislead you: I eat gluten. My grandmother and mother's balance of grace and hospitality inspired me to experiment in the kitchen and to share my table. But it is also because of these women that I LOVE bread. Regina Kogel can bake, and Sedonia Wagner before her, could also throw around some dough. (My sister Stacy and I even "choreographed" a celebratory dance for my mom's *kolache* baking!) I slung dough in a European-style bread bakery, and I believe in the health benefits of fermentation and sourdough bread, but I also believe a recipe can be gluten-free, healthy and satisfying to all.

This book celebrates the gluten-free, *whole* grains, from amaranth to wild rices. They're flavorful and nuanced, often steeped in ancient histories, and they're wholesome. But it's not all granola and birkenstocks (though I love both). We're going to fry foods for a new twist on tacos, but we're going to use heart-healthy oils. We're going to indulge in dessert, but we're going to use natural sweeteners, and we're going to use less of them. I'm a big believer in using the most natural version of an ingredient and enjoying it fully. This is the peace I have found with food.

My recipes are about more than buckwheat, more than millet. This collection is about living with nature, with the seasons, with respect for well-worn cutting boards and collecting flavors along the journey. My kitchen is an ode to the slow, intentional sort of endeavors. My site and this book are about sharing my time and my attention for the tiniest details with those I love. Now I want to share with *you*, and by extension, equip you to share with those *you* love.

Building the Gluten-Free Whole-Grain Pantry

The road to building my whole grain pantry was a literal uphill climb. When I first began baking, I wanted to develop a pantry that would enable me to respond to my sweet tooth's whims. One of the obvious staples was flour, so I went *all* in. I ordered a 5-pound (2.3-kg) case of Bob's Red Mill whole-grain flour from my local Whole Foods (do you know about case discounts?). Five pounds (2.3 kg) doesn't seem like a lot until you're walking, encumbered with a backpack of other groceries, 1½ miles (2.4 km) up Pittsburgh hills, which is to say, *vertical* climbs. These were the pre-Amazon, pre-Uber days, my friends.

Times are different now, and the world is at our fingertips. I would encourage you to approach this book as a way to build and expand your whole-grain pantry to include a gamut of gluten-free grains. Many of the recipes, especially when baking, include a mix of grains, for flavor and textural reasons, so there's an advantage to keeping an arsenal on hand (in airtight containers). Your expanded pantry will enable you to add variety and a host of health benefits to your diet. Alternatively, many of the recipes build off each other, so you can expand your pantry as you move through this book.

"New" ancient and gluten-free grains have been making some waves recently, but I stuck to the following grains because they are more readily available, but soon, you'll be a grainy geek too, and you can send me inspiration for all the new trending grains.

Amaranth

Amaranth was first cultivated in Mesoamerica 8,000 years ago and is believed to be the oldest grain, or more precisely, a "pseudo-cereal." It contains more protein than any other gluten-free grain (28.1 g per raw cup) and is an excellent source of lysine, an important amino acid missing in most grains. Amaranth has a slightly nutty flavor and a creamier, porridge-like consistency. I don't recommend it for grain bowls unless it's cooked with another grain such as wild rice. Amaranth really shines when used in soups, such as my Creamy Amaranth Corn Chowder (page 146) and my Smoky Cream of Tomato Soup (page 144), or when soaked, blended and baked, like in the amaranth flatbreads (page 62).

Buckwheat Groats/Kasha (Roasted Buckwheat Groats)

Though they are technically the hulled *seeds* of the buckwheat plant (a relative of rhubarb), buckwheat groats behave like a grain and are categorized as such. Buckwheat supports the healthy digestion and absorption of nutrients in food, and each ¼ cup (43 g) of buckwheat contains 6 grams of protein and 8 percent of your recommended daily value of iron. Buckwheat has a strong, earthy and nearly bitter flavor profile akin to a hoppy beer. When used in baking, buckwheat yields a denser crumb, so mix buckwheat with other flours, like millet, for the Cranberry & Goat Cheese–Swirled Sheet Pan Pancake (page 57). Buckwheat groats add a nutty crunch that lends itself to granolas (page 34 and page 36) or as a sweet, nougat-like crunch on the Twin Bing Cherry–Chocolate Popsicles (page 184). When cooked al dente, buckwheat groats add a wheaty berry-like crunch to salads like the Summer Harvest Salad (page 162).

Cornmeal

Fresh corn is usually classified as a vegetable, but dried corn (including popcorn) is considered a grain. Cornmeal is the grain that offers the most vitamin A. It's also high in antioxidants and carotenoids, which help maintain eye health. In Central and South American culinary traditions, corn is often "nixtamalized"—soaked in an alkaline solution (often limewater)—then drained and made into masa flour, tortillas and other foods with better health attributes. Put this theory to work with the Cornmeal Sopes (page 121). Avoid "degermed" cornmeal, as that means the super-nutritious germ has been removed. The buttery sweetness of cornmeal lends itself to sweeter dishes like The Beekeeper's Breakfast Bowl or as a complementary flour in the Big-Batch Multigrain Pancake Mix (page 50). The coarser texture of cornmeal adds a crunch in recipes like the Cheddar-Jalapeño Waffles (page 58) or as a batter in the Spicy Cod & Chorizo Bake (page 109).

Millet

Millet is not just one grain, but rather the name applied to several small-seeded grains from the *Poaceae* grass family. In the United States, it is most associated with birdseed, but we'd be remiss to leave this grain "to the birds." Millet is rich in antioxidants, and it's especially high in magnesium, which helps maintain muscle and nerve function. Millet is also beneficial for controlling diabetes and inflammation. It has a rich, buttery aroma when cooking, and its texture ranges from a creamy porridge in the Chai-Spiced Pumpkin Pie Bowl (page 25), to a more pronounced texture like the Marseille Millet Bowl (page 80).

Oats (Steel-Cut, Rolled, Quick-Cooking)

Oats are one of the more approachable gluten-free grains. Chances are you grew up with a flavor variety pack of Quaker Oats in your pantry. Steel-cut, rolled and instant/quick oats all come from the whole oat groat, but they undergo different processes that mainly affect the cooking times and texture. The resulting nutritional profiles are relatively the same. Instant oats, or quick oats, are pre-cooked, dried, rolled and pressed thinner to cook more quickly, but I save that variety for nostalgia, since the resulting texture tends to be mushier. Rolled oats, the flattened form of the grain, add a creamy texture and a sweetness to my Go-To Multigrain Hot Cereal (page 18). Steel-cut oats, the chewier, nuttier whole oat kernel, requires slower cooking but yields a porridge with more bite for recipes like the Savory Oats with Maple Sausage & Cherry Sauce (page 69). Oats are naturally gluten-free, but they are often processed with wheat, so be sure to buy oats from a gluten-free facility if you need to. Eating oats may help reduce the risk of diabetes, control weight and keep you feeling fuller longer.

Quinoa (White, Red, Black, Tricolor)

Quinoa is considered a "pseudo-cereal," since it is actually a seed, but it behaves like a grain. Quinoa exploded on the health scene because it has a very high protein content, and it's one of the only plant foods that's a *complete* protein, which means it offers all the essential amino acids in a healthy balance. It's also the grain with the most potassium, which helps control blood pressure. It's pronounced texture makes it a counterpart to rice and a grain bowl staple. When cooked and toasted, quinoa can add a crunch like in the A Chocoholic's Brunch Salad (page 66) or a batter that mimics the texture of frying in the Oven-"Fried" Chicken (page 94). You won't find quinoa flour in this recipe collection because it's cost prohibitive and yields a very pronounced grassy taste that overrides the sweetness of dessert.

Rice (Brown Rice, Brown Basmati, Emperor's/Black Rice, Himalayan Red Rice, Purple Thai Rice, Wild Rice)

There are over 40,000 different known varieties of rice, but only a few of those are commercially available. With higher levels of vitamins and minerals, the whole grain varieties are the healthier choice. These whole grain options come in a range of colors and grain lengths, so it's worth experimenting and alternating what you buy. Black rice, dubbed "Emperor's rice," was once reserved for Chinese emperors only, to ensure their longevity. It's rich in antioxidant pigments that give the rice its unique hue. Wild rice is a good source of fiber, folate, magnesium, phosphorus, manganese, zinc, vitamin B6 and niacin. Rice's flavor varies by kind. If you're pairing rice with other strong flavors, pick a more intense variety, like the Emperor's rice in The Vegan Gaucho Grain Bowl (page 78), which also adds a bold color contrast. Brown rice flour is one of my favorites, yielding a crumb and flavor similar to a whole-wheat flour. It's the star of the Apple Season Layer Cake (page 175).

Sorghum

More often associated with sweeteners in Southern cuisine, whole-grain sorghum originated in Africa thousands of years ago. It then spread through the Middle East and Asia, via ancient trade routes, traveling to the Arabian Peninsula, India and China along the Silk Road. Today sorghum remains a staple food in India and Africa. Sorghum doesn't have an inedible hull like many other grains, so its outer layers remain intact, thereby retaining the majority of its nutrients. Sorghum maintains a pronounced texture after cooking, so use it as an accent in salads like the Watermelon-Sorghum Salad (page 161), or dishes that need a bit of contrast like the Eggplant Rollatini (page 118). Sorghum flour is a light and mild flour often sold as "sweet white sorghum." Sorghum and oat flour work very interchangeably.

⚡ Teff

Hailing from Ethiopia and Eritrea, the word *teff* is often assumed to be related to the word "lost" in Amharic—because of the tiny size of its seeds (less than 1 mm in diameter—similar to a poppy seed). Since the grain is too small to process, it's always eaten in whole grain form and boasts the highest calcium content of the whole grains. Many of Ethiopia's long-distance runners attribute their sustained energy and successes to the health benefits of teff. Whole-grain teff behaves a lot like cornmeal, so use it as you would a polenta like in the Teff Polenta Triangles with Peach Ceviche (page 129) or as a creamy breakfast porridge in the Raw Cacao Bowl (page 26). As a flour, teff is one of my go-to gluten-free substitutions. It's mild and earthy with a hint of sweetness like molasses. It yields a brown color and flavor similar to whole-wheat flour, and its higher protein content helps add structure to baked goods like the Maple-Sweetened Pecan Pie Bars (page 188) or the Big-Batch Mulitgrain Pancake Mix (page 50).

A Few Additional Pantry Staples

Arrowroot Flour/Starch/Powder

Arrowroot is a very fine white powder derived from a tropical, perennial herb *Maranta arundinacea*. It's used in gluten-free cooking and baking for a variety of reasons. It yields a better crumb, aids in the rising process and helps bind ingredients together, much like an egg, without altering the flavor of the recipe. You can find arrowroot in your baking aisle, or online and definitely via Bob's Red Mill, who shares one possible story as to the origin of the name. Some stories claim the South American Arawak Indians used the arrowroot plant medicinally to draw out toxins from poisoned arrow wounds. Take that tidbit or leave it, but it could be a fun fact to share with other baking nerds. The choice is up to you, my friends.

Psyllium Husk/Powder

Psyllium husk is a fiber derived from a shrub-like herb called *Plantago ovata*. Each plant can produce up to 15,000 tiny, gel-coated seeds, from which psyllium husk is derived. It's the same fiber used in products like Metamucil, so you'll likely find the husk or ground powder version in the health foods and wellness section of a natural grocer as opposed to the baking aisle. Psyllium has become popular in gluten-free baking for its egg-like, binding abilities. Psyllium husk and/or powder work as an alternative to xanthum gum, which is commonly found in gluten-free flour mixes but can be difficult for some to digest.

A Note About Oils

Most recipes in this book will call for avocado oil or a "high-heat oil." Like the fruit itself, avocado oil is a superfood. It's full of healthy fats, but unlike other nutrient-dense oils, it has a high smoke point (520°F [271°C]), meaning it won't lose nutrients or flavor at high temperatures. Avocado oil has become more readily available with more economic options at stores like Costco. Since it also works well for dressings, it's worth keeping in your pantry for everyday use.

Gluten-Free Grains Cooking Guide

It's best to store your grains in an airtight, glass container, which means the instructions from the packaging will most likely land in the recycling bin. As you work your way through this book and become familiar with these grains, their cooking ratios will become second nature, but in the meantime, dog ear this page for a quick reference.

Name		Description	Yield
Amaranth		Bring 3 cups (720 ml) of water to a boil in a pot. Add 1 cup (128 g) of amaranth. Cover, reduce the heat and simmer until the water is absorbed, about 20 minutes. Fluff with a fork.	2⅔ cups (453 g)
Brown Rice (long grain)		Bring 1 cup (128 g) of brown rice and 2 cups (480 ml) of water or stock to a boil. Reduce the heat to low. Cover and simmer for 40 to 45 minutes.	4 cups (681 g)
Buckwheat Groats		Combine 1 cup (128 g) of buckwheat groats and 2 cups (480 ml) of water in a pot. Bring to a boil; cover, reduce the heat to simmer and cook until tender, about 10 minutes. Drain off any excess liquid. If using in a salad, rinse with cold water and drain well.	2½ cups (425 g)
Cornmeal/Corn Grits (Polenta)		Bring 3 cups (720 ml) of water and ½ teaspoon of salt to a boil. Add 1 cup (170 g) of cornmeal/corn grits and reduce the heat. Cook slowly for about 5 minutes, stirring occasionally. Remove from the heat, cover and let stand for a couple minutes.	2½ cups (425 g)
Millet, Hulled		Bring 2 cups (480 ml) of water or stock to a boil in a pot for pilaf style; 3 cups (720 ml) for a porridge. Add 1 cup (170 g) of rinsed and drained millet; cover, reduce the heat to medium-low and simmer until all of the water is absorbed, about 20 minutes.	2½ cups (425 g)

Name		Description	Yield
Oats, Rolled		Bring 2 cups (480 ml) of water and ¼ teaspoon of salt to a boil. Add 1 cup (80 g) of rolled oats, reduce the heat and cook for 10 to 20 minutes (depending on the consistency you desire). Stir occasionally. Cover and remove from the heat and let stand for a few minutes.	2 cups (160 g)
Oats, Steel-Cut		Bring 4 cups (960 ml) of water to boil. Add 1 cup (160 g) of steel-cut oats. When the porridge is smooth and beginning to thicken, reduce the heat and simmer uncovered for about 30 minutes, stirring occasionally.	4 cups (643 g)
Quinoa		Bring 2 cups (480 ml) of water or stock to a boil. Add 1 cup (170 g) of rinsed and drained quinoa, and return to a boil. Cover, reduce the heat to medium and let simmer until the water is absorbed, about 12 minutes. Remove from the heat, fluff, cover and let stand for 15 minutes.	3½–4 cups (596–681 g)
Sorghum		Combine 3 cups (720 ml) of water or stock and 1 cup (170 g) of rinsed and drained sorghum in a pot with a tight-fitting lid. Bring to a boil. Cover, reduce the heat to low and let simmer until tender, about 50 to 60 minutes. Drain any excess water.	3½ cups (596 g)
Teff		Add ½ cup (85 g) of teff grain to 2 cups (480 ml) of boiling water or stock. Cover, reduce the heat to low and simmer 15 to 20 minutes or until the water is absorbed. Stir occasionally.	1½ cups (255 g)
Wild Rice		Bring 1 cup (170 g) of wild rice and 2½ cups (590 ml) of liquid to a boil. Reduce the heat to low. Cover and simmer for 40 to 50 minutes.	3 cups (511 g)

Source: Whole Grains Council

Breakfast

A Healthy Whole-Grain Start

One New Year's Eve, I made a resolution to eat a different breakfast each day for a month. I needed something big and defined to shake me from bad habits. I was all too often sleep deprived and pressed for time, which led to skipping breakfast entirely or deferring to the pastries at the coffee shop. Even if your local morning coffee stop has a gluten-free option, don't assume it's the healthiest choice. There's often nutritionally bland flours, binders, gums and lots of refined sugars lurking behind the guise of health.

There's at least two week's worth of breakfast ideas in this section, so you can shake up your breakfast routine. Plus, through the power of whole grain eating, you can reduce the risk of heart disease, stroke, cancer, diabetes and obesity. Go ahead and pat yourself on the back, because that's demonstrating a *lot* of responsibility, all before noon.

But that doesn't mean you'll be eating cold bundles of shredded grain. On chilly mornings, there's nothing quite like a warm, creamy bowl of hot cereal. We're turning pumpkin pie into a healthy breakfast bowl (Chai-Spiced Pumpkin Pie Bowl, page 25), and we're adding even more grains to our oatmeal for a high-protein bowl that will fill you until lunchtime (Go-To Multigrain Hot Cereal, page 18). Drizzled with infused honeys or a dollop of chamomile whipped cream (The Beekeeper's Breakfast Bowl, page 29) and paired with Iced Oat-Milk Lattes (page 46), these are café-worthy combos from the comfort of home.

There are recipes to change your mindset and shake up your palate. Think fried rice for breakfast with a hint of sweetness and a golden, turmeric poached egg (Bacon Fried Rice, page 30). There are savory, rosy-colored beet cakes to take the place of bagels (Multigrain Beet Breakfast Patties, page 22).

For rushed mornings when you need a breakfast on the go, you'll be prepared with savory multigrain muffins (Caramelized Onion & Mushroom Multigrain Muffins, page 21), or pack a parfait with chocolate quinoa crunchers (Chocolate-Quinoa Cruncher Parfaits, page 33) and you'll enjoy a chocolatey dose of potassium, which helps control blood pressure. There's rose-colored and flavored granola (Rose-Colored Roasted Beet & Rose Water Granola, page 34) to awaken your senses and matcha tea cakes (Blackberry Matcha Tea Cakes, page 38) for slower mornings, so let's get started!

Go-To Multigrain Hot Cereal

AMARANTH, BUCKWHEAT, MILLET, OATS, QUINOA | MAKES 15 SERVINGS

Remember when kids would mix all the sodas from the fountain machine into one cup and think they were *so* rebellious? This is my adult, grainy version of that game. This is a clean sweep of the gluten-free offerings at my co-op's bulk bins, and the resulting hot cereal is creamy, subtly sweet and so filling, you might need a reminder to eat lunch. Topping your bowl with your favorite oatmeal flavorings or a drizzle of the oat milk and infused honey from the oat-milk latte recipe on page 46 is an easy way to add a lot of flavor to this breakfast bowl.

This hearty mix forms the base of the Caramelized Onion & Mushroom Multigrain Muffins (page 21) and Multigrain Beet Breakfast Patties (page 22) for more multigrain starts to your day. As an added bonus, if you buy bigger quantities of these grains, your pantry will be stocked and ready for many more of the subsequent recipes in this book.

Big Batch Cereal Mix
1 cup (190 g) amaranth
1 cup (170 g) buckwheat groats
1 cup (206 g) millet
1 cup (99 g) rolled oats
1 cup (177 g) quinoa
1 cup (160 g) flaxseeds
1 cup (140 g) sunflower seeds
½ cup (80 g) chia seeds

Single Serving of Hot Cereal
½ cup (100 g) multigrain cereal mix
1½ cups (360 ml) water

For the big batch, combine everything in an airtight glass container.

For a single serving, combine the water and the cereal mix in a saucepan over medium-high heat. Bring the mixture to a boil, then reduce the heat, cover and simmer for 20 minutes. Uncover and stir, and continue to simmer uncovered until the cereal mix is thickened and the water has been absorbed, 5 to 10 minutes. Top with your favorite flavorings and serve warm.

SOME OF MY FAVORITE FLAVOR COMBINATIONS

+ *Apples, cinnamon, nutmeg and cardamom*
+ *Walnuts and a touch of brown sugar*
+ *Blueberries and lemon zest*
+ *Cranberries, pears and honey*
+ *Full-fat coconut milk and bananas*

TIPS & TRICKS
Want to give a thoughtful gift to a new neighbor, a new mom or a host(ess)? Seal this cereal in a pretty mason jar, add some twine, attach the instructions and voila!

Caramelized Onion & Mushroom Multigrain Muffins

AMARANTH, BUCKWHEAT, MILLET, OATS, QUINOA | VEGETARIAN | MAKES 18 MUFFINS

One of my best friends and I spent three weeks traveling the West Coast together. We started calling ourselves "best sharing friends," as we "halfsied" our way through menus in major foodie cities like Portland and San Francisco. The one area where we diverged though? Breakfast! The girl does *not* share my sweet tooth's "need" for pastries and doughnuts in the morning.

This muffin is for you, Lindsey, but it's also for all the "Lindseys" in *your* life—those who want caramelized onion, mushrooms and cheddar for a savory start to their days. The whole grain millet creates a seedy crunch, and the millet flour lends a buttery flavor much like a cornbread. Of course, if you lean to the sweeter side of breakfast, you can always save these to dip into Creamy Amaranth Corn Chowder (page 146) or pair with the Pickle-Brined Oven-"Fried" Chicken Tenders (page 94).

1 cup (170 g) Go-To Multigrain Hot Cereal (page 18)

1¼ cups (295 ml) buttermilk

1 tbsp (15 g) unsalted butter

1 red onion, peeled and diced

12 oz (340 g) portobello mushrooms, chopped

1 cup (130 g) millet flour

1 tsp (4 g) baking powder

1 tsp (4 g) baking soda

1 tsp (5 g) salt

½ tsp crushed black pepper

⅓ cup (78 ml) avocado oil

4 eggs

1½ cups (195 g) finely shredded Mexican cheese blend, divided

Zest of 1 lemon

1 cup (340 g) chopped kale

¾ oz (21 g) chives, chopped

In a large bowl, combine the cereal mix and buttermilk, and set aside to soak for at least 20 minutes, or ideally, overnight.

After the grains have soaked and you're ready to prepare the muffins, start by placing a skillet over medium heat to melt the butter. Add the diced onion to the pan and stir to coat with butter. Caramelize the onion, cooking for 20 to 30 minutes, stirring every 5 to 10 minutes to prevent sticking. If the onions get too dark or stick too much in the process, you can add a little water and continue to cook.

Once the onion has caramelized, add the mushrooms and cook until the mushrooms are browned, stirring frequently, about 5 minutes. Remove from the heat and set aside.

Preheat the oven to 400°F (204°C). Grease muffin tin(s) and/or line with muffin cups.

Sift the millet flour, baking powder, baking soda, salt and pepper into a large mixing bowl. Whisk gently to combine. Set aside.

Pour the soaked cereal mixture into the bowl of a stand mixer. Add the oil, and beat on low. Add the eggs one at a time, scraping down the bowl with a spatula. Mix in ¾ cup (98 g) of cheese and the lemon zest.

Add the flour mixture and beat until just combined, scraping down the bowl with a spatula.

Fold in the caramelized onion–mushroom mixture, chopped kale and chives. Divide the batter equally among the prepared muffin cups. Top the muffins with the remaining ¾ cup (98 g) of cheese.

Bake for 30 to 35 minutes, or until tops of the muffins are golden and a toothpick inserted in the center comes out clean. Let cool in pan on a wire rack until cool to the touch, then transfer to the rack to cool completely. Store muffins in an airtight container in the fridge.

Multigrain Beet Breakfast Patties

AMARANTH, BUCKWHEAT, MILLET, OATS, QUINOA, TEFF │ VEGETARIAN OPTION │
MAKES ABOUT 18 PATTIES (6 SERVINGS)

Beets are to my kitchen as fingerpaints were to my childhood. They're colorful, messy outlets for creativity and stained fingers, so roll up your sleeves and prepare to play with your food. You're about to paint the Go-To Multigrain Hot Cereal (page 18) a rosy shade of beet!

These multigrain Beet Breakfast Patties are similar in texture to a falafel. Think of these colorful patties as a healthy carrier for all your favorite savory morning ingredients. For a vegetarian option, top with a poached or sunny side up egg. To get more mileage from a batch, you can also experiment shaping the patties like a meatball, then adding them to wraps, salads or grain bowls with tahini dressing, so you'll have your lunch covered too.

Beet Patties

2 cups (322 g) grated zucchini

½ tsp salt

1½ cups (355 ml) water

½ cup (85 g) Go-To Multigrain Hot Cereal (page 18)

2 medium beets, peeled

1 cup (120 g) grated fresh Parmigiano-Reggiano or pecorino cheese

½ tsp garlic powder

½ tsp onion powder

¼ cup (13 g) chopped fresh dill

1 cup (130 g) teff flour

1 egg, beaten

3 tbsp (45 ml) avocado oil

To Serve

Smoked salmon

Herbed goat cheese or Greek yogurt with herbs

Capers

Fresh dill and chives

To make the beet patties, place the zucchini in a colander, and toss with salt. Let stand for 10 minutes, then wring the zucchini dry with a paper towel. In the meantime, prepare the multigrain cereal.

Combine the water and the cereal mix in a saucepan over medium-high heat. Bring to a boil, then reduce the heat, cover and simmer for 20 minutes. Uncover and stir, and continue to simmer uncovered until the cereal mix is thickened and the water has been absorbed, 5 to 10 minutes. Remove from the heat, and cool completely.

While the cereal cools, pulse the peeled beets in a food processor until finely diced. Transfer to a large mixing bowl. Add the cooled cereal, the grated zucchini, cheese, garlic powder, onion powder, fresh dill, teff flour and the beaten egg. Stir until it is thoroughly combined and the mixture begins to hold together (it will still be somewhat wet).

Heat the avocado oil in a skillet over medium heat. Shape the mixture into balls—slightly larger than a golf ball—and add 3 to 4 portions to the pan. Cook for 1 minute, then flatten slightly with a spatula. Cook for 2 to 3 more minutes until crisped, then flip and cook for another 3 to 4 minutes. Transfer the breakfast patties to a paper towel–lined sheet pan.

To serve, top with smoked salmon, herbed goat cheese or Greek yogurt, a few capers and herbs.

Chai-Spiced Pumpkin Pie Bowl

BUCKWHEAT GROATS, MILLET, ROLLED OATS | VEGETARIAN, VEGAN OPTION | MAKES 4–6 SERVINGS

Annoyed that I wouldn't eat *anything* at family gatherings because I deemed it too unhealthy, my sister told me to find a healthy dessert recipe I would actually eat. These were the *very* early days of the Internet. Wholesome desserts were harder to find, but I managed to find a whole grain pumpkin pie recipe. On Thanksgiving day, Tosha rather indignantly presented the pie. Grateful for her efforts, I enthusiastically took my first bite, and it was . . . TERRIBLE!

That pie was so heavily spiced, I immediately needed a glass of water. My mom, the experienced baker, pinpointed the error: the nutmeg. What should have been ¼ teaspoon was listed as ¼ cup (30 g). I couldn't muster another bite, not even to appease my irritated sister. Not wanting to waste it, my mom crushed up that horrid pie, added some magic and baked it into the most delicious, never-to-be-repeated pumpkin bread, which I think about every fall. This pumpkin pie bowl tastes like an indulgent bite of pie with just the right amount of nutmeg. Plus, both pumpkin and millet are fiber-rich ingredients, so you won't crash before lunchtime.

Millet

1 cup (170 g) millet, rinsed and drained

2 cups (480 ml) water

1 chai tea bag

¼ tsp salt

1 cup (180 g) pumpkin purée

3 tbsp (45 ml) maple syrup

1 tsp (3 g) cinnamon

¼ tsp ground cardamom

¼ tsp ground nutmeg

Streusel Topping

½ cup (60 g) chopped pecans

½ cup (40 g) rolled oats

¼ cup (43 g) buckwheat groats

3 tbsp (45 ml) maple syrup

1 tsp vanilla extract

½ tsp cinnamon

¼ tsp nutmeg

To Serve

Plain or vanilla Greek yogurt (omit for vegan option)

Maple syrup

To make the millet, heat a saucepan over medium heat. Add the millet, and toast lightly until dry and a shade darker, about 3 to 5 minutes, stirring to prevent burning. Add the water, chai tea bag and salt. Give the ingredients a good stir, then bring to a boil. Reduce to a simmer, cover and cook for approximately 15 minutes, until the grain has puffed up and absorbed the liquid. Remove from the heat, and discard the tea bag. Give it a good stir, then cover and allow to sit to fully absorb any remaining liquid, about 10 minutes. Uncover the millet, and fluff with a fork. Then stir in the pumpkin purée, maple syrup, cinnamon, cardamom and nutmeg.

To make the streusel topping, heat a sauté pan over medium-high heat. Add the chopped pecans, rolled oats and buckwheat groats. Toast for 1 to 2 minutes until golden brown and fragrant (the pecans will release oils), tossing or stirring to prevent burning. Remove from the heat, and add the maple syrup, vanilla, cinnamon and nutmeg. Stir to combine, then transfer to a bowl to prevent any further browning.

To serve, divide the millet amongst your serving bowls, top with a dollop of yogurt and a sprinkle of the streusel. Drizzle with maple syrup, and enjoy!

> TIPS & TRICKS
> *The streusel recipe yields more than you need for just the pumpkin pie bowls, so you'll have a few more breakfast options. It's a tasty topper for yogurt, or serve it with milk like granola. For a creamier, even more pie-like texture, try this recipe with rolled oats instead of millet.*

"You're No Quitter" Raw Cacao Bowl

Teff │ Vegetarian, Vegan Option │ Makes 1 serving

"I'd give up chocolate, but I'm no quitter." I painted this on wooden plaques to give my mom and sisters one year for a particularly crafty Christmas. Years later, I dare say this has become my mantra. I will almost *always* try to "chocolatize" a recipe, but with this raw cacao teff bowl, I may be onto something!

Teff is tiny (it's the smallest grain, roughly the size of a chia seed), but it is mighty (a great source of protein, manganese, iron and calcium). However, the real magic for us ladies is that adding teff to our diets can help us cut back the inflammation, bloating, cramping and muscle pain associated with PMS. Teff is high in phosphorus, so it naturally helps to balance hormones (i.e., *the Lord's work*).

Simply put, eating this chocolate bowl, right when you might be craving chocolate anyway, can be beneficial in negating those symptoms. So this bowl might keep you from quitting other activities (but not chocolate, *never* quit chocolate). All things considered, this is the *one* recipe I give you permission not to share.

Teff Porridge

1 cup (240 ml) water

2 tbsp (14 g) raw cacao powder

Pinch of sea salt

¼ cup (43 g) whole grain teff

To Serve

Greek yogurt (substitute coconut cream for vegan option)

Sliced kumquats and/or other citrus

Orange zest

Raw cacao nibs

Sea salt

Honey

To make the teff porridge, in a saucepan over medium-high heat, bring the water, raw cacao powder and the sea salt to boil, whisking to dissolve the cacao. Add the teff, cover, reduce the heat to low and simmer, stirring occasionally to help the mixture thicken and prevent sticking. Simmer for 15 to 20 minutes, or until the liquid is absorbed. Remove from the heat, and transfer to a serving bowl.

To serve, top with a dollop of Greek yogurt, sliced kumquats, orange zest, cacao nibs and a sprinkle of sea salt. Drizzle with honey, and give everything a good stir to mix the flavors.

> ### Tips & Tricks
> *Raw cacao powder comes from cold-pressing unroasted cocoa beans, so the enzymes and nutrients remain intact, unlike cocoa, which has been roasted. Raw cacao powder does tend to be a little more expensive, but in recent years, it has become more readily available with more affordable options, including Trader Joe's. In a pinch, you can substitute cocoa.*

The Beekeeper's Breakfast Bowl

CORNMEAL | VEGETARIAN | MAKES 2 SERVINGS (PERFECT FOR YOU *and* A BEEKEEPER)

My grandparents had a sweet deal with local beekeepers (pun intended). The beekeepers used my grandparents' South Dakota farmland in exchange for honey, but over the years, the honey accumulated beyond demand. When I discovered my grandfather was feeding the caramel-like, double-spun, clover honey to his calves, I immediately started packing! Upon returning to my own kitchen, I doled out the liquid gold rations with all the generosity of a bread-line worker.

Years later, I fell in love with my farmer/beekeeper, and I began to regard bees with a whole new level of understanding and respect. This breakfast bowl celebrates the hardworking bees and their keepers. The base is cornmeal—an ode to the crops my grandparents grew on their farm—topped with honey-caramelized pears and plums, the fruits I picked from our trees as a kid.

The more indulgent element here is the chamomile and calendula-infused whipped cream. For the best flavor, start that step the night before, and infuse overnight. The result is earthy and subtly floral. To really support your area's bees, be sure to use a local honey and top with bee pollen, which contains almost all of the nutrients required by the human body to thrive. It's a superfood start to the day and can even help combat seasonal allergies.

Chamomile-Calendula Whipped Cream
1 cup (240 ml) heavy cream
1 heaping tbsp (2 g) dried chamomile
1 heaping tbsp (2 g) dried calendula
1 tsp (5 ml) vanilla extract

Polenta
1½ cups (355 ml) water
1½ cups (355 ml) buttermilk
¼ tsp salt
1 cup (170 g) coarse cornmeal/corn grits

Honey-Caramelized Fruit
1 tbsp (15 g) butter
⅓ cup (78 ml) honey
1 sprig rosemary, chopped
1 pear, sliced into ¼-inch (6-mm) slices
1 plum, sliced into ¼-inch (6-mm) slices

To Serve
Bee pollen

To make the whipped cream, in a saucepan over medium heat, bring the cream to a simmer. Remove from the heat, add the chamomile and calendula, and set aside to infuse for at least 20 minutes. I like to leave it in the fridge overnight for maximum flavor. Once infused and cooled, strain and use a stand mixer to beat the infused cream and vanilla extract until stiff peaks form. Keep chilled until ready to serve. You'll probably have a little extra, so you can save some for dessert.

To make the polenta, bring the water, buttermilk and salt to a boil. The buttermilk adds a tangy, yogurt-like flavor to the polenta. If that doesn't sound appealing, simply double the water quantity. Add the cornmeal and reduce the heat. Cook slowly for about 5 minutes, stirring occasionally to prevent sticking. Remove from the heat, cover and let stand for a couple of minutes. Meanwhile, caramelize the fruit.

To make the fruit, heat the butter in a large skillet over medium heat. Add the honey and cook, stirring, until the honey is dissolved, 1 to 2 minutes. Add the rosemary, pear and plum slices, and continue to cook, stirring occasionally, until soft and just golden. For fruit that's sweetened but still firm, this should take about 3 to 5 minutes, or 5 to 10 minutes for deeper caramelization. Reserve any extra liquid for drizzling over the polenta.

To serve, top the polenta with the fruit, and drizzle with extra honey liquid from the pan. Top with the chamomile-calendula whipped cream and bee pollen.

> **TIPS & TRICKS**
> *Your local co-op is the best option for sourcing loose chamomile and calendula, but if you can't find them, you can always use the contents of a chamomile tea bag, or simply sweeten the cream with honey. You can find bee pollen in health food stores or online.*

Bacon Fried Rice with Peas, Parm & Turmeric Poached Eggs

BROWN RICE | VEGETARIAN OPTION | MAKES 4 SERVINGS

Perfect for using leftover rice from last night's dinner or stealing from your grain bowl meal prepping, this bowl packs the creamy, cheesiness of a classic Italian pasta dish with the power of whole grains. It also takes a cue from my Korean college roommates. They'd wake up early and prepare savory spreads that put my granola bars to shame. This breakfast bowl is for you, my savory-leaning friends, but the peas and fresh mint add just a touch of sweetness because I couldn't resist.

Brown rice is a slow-release carbohydrate, which means this bowl will help your body maintain blood sugar levels and prevent a mid-morning crash. For a vegetarian version, or for the sake of variety, skip the bacon and sauté some portobello mushrooms. The turmeric poached egg adds a little spice and warmth, but it's also a visual feast—isn't that yellow *pretty*? If the notion of creating a cloud-like poached egg before your coffee kicks in feels too intimidating, stick to the classic sunny side up egg, and your day will still be golden.

Fried Rice

1 (10-oz [283-g]) bag frozen peas
2 tbsp (30 ml) avocado oil, plus more for drizzling
½ cup (120 ml) heavy cream
½ cup (20 g) chopped mint leaves
1 clove garlic
1 lemon
½ cup (90 g) grated Parmesan
Freshly ground black pepper
4 slices thick-cut bacon, chopped
1 shallot, diced
3 cups (483 g) cooked brown rice

Turmeric Poached Eggs

¼ cup (60 ml) distilled white vinegar
2 tsp (6 g) ground turmeric
4 large eggs

To make the fried rice, bring a saucepan with enough water to cover the peas. Bring to a boil over high heat. When the water has reached a rolling boil, add the frozen peas, and cook until the peas are tender and start to float, about 3 minutes. Remove from the heat, and strain the water. Add the oil, heavy cream and chopped mint. Using a microplane, finely grate the garlic clove and zest the lemon into the pea mixture. Add the Parmesan, and stir to combine. Season with the black pepper, and set aside.

Heat a sauté pan over medium heat. Add the chopped bacon and shallot, and cook for 4 to 6 minutes, until the bacon reaches your desired level of crispiness and shallots are translucent, stirring frequently to prevent sticking. Stir in the cooked brown rice and continue to cook until the bacon and shallots are evenly distributed. Continue to cook, stirring to prevent sticking. If you need to add oil, push all of the rice to one side of the pan, add the oil, then redistribute. Cook for another 3 to 5 minutes, until the rice is browned and slightly crispy. Reduce the heat to low, then stir in the pea mixture and cover while you poach the eggs.

To make the turmeric poached eggs, pour 2 inches (5 cm) of water into a large saucepan, and bring to a boil. Reduce the heat and keep the water at a gentle simmer (there should only be small bubbles rising). Add the vinegar and turmeric. Crack an egg into a small bowl. Stir the water to create a gentle whirlpool, then slowly tip the egg into the center of the liquid. Cook for 3 to 4 minutes, until the white is set. Use a slotted spoon to lift the egg and transfer to a paper towel–lined plate to drain. Repeat with the remaining eggs.

> ### TIPS & TRICKS
> *You can add more than one egg to the liquid to speed up the process, just wait about 30 seconds in between eggs. Try this recipe with a variety of rices, or try a multigrain mix and throw other leftovers into the recipe like buckwheat groats, quinoa or sorghum.*

Chocolate-Quinoa Cruncher Parfaits

QUINOA | VEGETARIAN | MAKES 4–6 SERVINGS

Even though my mom so frequently put homemade, hot breakfasts on the table, as a child of the '80s and '90s, I ate my fair share of sugary cereals. I shudder when I think about the mini cookies and French toasts and their long lists of ingredients, but dang, if I still don't crave something sweet in the mornings!

This recipe lets you embrace your inner child in a much healthier way (or feed your actual child in a much healthier way). You start by cooking quinoa with raw cacao, a sweet treat but a far cry from sugary cereals. Then, bake the quinoa in the oven for a bit of crunch. The resulting texture is similar to a granola but not *quite* as crunchy. The milder crunch works best as a yogurt parfait, or over fruit, rather than in milk.

Chocolate-Quinoa Crunchers

¾ cup (128 g) uncooked quinoa

2½ tbsp (37 ml) melted coconut oil, divided

1½ cups (355 ml) filtered water

2 tbsp (23 g) raw cacao

½ cup (85 g) whole almonds, roughly chopped

½ cup (60 g) whole pecans, roughly chopped

¼ cup (40 g) golden flaxseeds

2 tbsp (30 ml) honey

1 tbsp (15 ml) vanilla extract

1 tsp (5 g) sea salt

Parfaits

Greek yogurt, to serve

Fruit or fruit compote, to serve

To make the quinoa crunchers, pour the quinoa into a fine mesh strainer, and rinse for 2 minutes with cool water, swishing and mixing with your hand to rinse thoroughly. Drain.

Heat ½ tablespoon (7 g) of coconut oil in a saucepan over medium-high heat. Add the drained quinoa, and toast until any remaining water has evaporated, 1 to 2 minutes. Add the water and raw cacao, and bring the mixture to a boil. Reduce the heat, cover and simmer for 15 minutes. Remove from the heat, let stand, covered, for 5 minutes, then fluff with a fork, and set aside.

Preheat the oven to 350°F (177°C). Line a baking sheet with parchment paper.

In a large mixing bowl, combine the remaining coconut oil, almonds, pecans, flaxseeds, honey, vanilla and sea salt. Stir in the cooked quinoa. Spread the mixture over the prepared baking sheet, and bake for 40 to 50 minutes, stirring every 15 minutes, until crisp but not burnt. Remove from the oven and allow to cool before storing in an airtight container.

To make the parfaits, combine the yogurt and your favorite fruit or fruit compote, and top with the chocolate quinoa crunchers.

> ### TIPS & TRICKS
> *Pair this recipe with a tart rhubarb compote when rhubarb season comes around, and for a tangy variation, try adding lemon zest to your yogurt. Both contrast the lightly sweetened crunchers nicely. Or, for more of a cooling ice-cream-sundae vibe, try adding fresh mint to your yogurt.*

Rose-Colored Roasted Beet & Rose Water Granola

BUCKWHEAT GROATS, OATS | MAKES 5½ CUPS (937 G)

We've matured. We've grown up and made healthier choices. We've parted ways with Lucky Charms and largely, the cereal aisle, but does that mean our breakfast cereal can't leave our milk colorful? Isn't that last sip of flavor-infused milk the reason to eat cereal in the first place?

This rosy, beet-sweetened, lightly floral bowl is an elevated return to childhood. You're eating vegetables for breakfast—if that doesn't merit a gold star . . . ! If you want to put on cartoons while you eat, or dedicate your bowl to the most infamous beet farmer, Dwight Schrute, and rewatch *The Office* in your pjs for the 100th time, I say, "Get me a bowl, and save me a seat!" Serve this granola with milk, maybe even *extra* milk because that last sip is quite the treat.

1½ cups (255 g) hulled buckwheat groats

1½ cups (121 g) rolled oats

½ cup (63 g) pepitas

½ cup (63 g) sunflower seeds

½ cup (80 g) flaxseeds

¼ cup (43 g) flax meal

1 tsp (5 g) sea salt

3 medium beets, roasted and peeled

½ cup (120 ml) melted coconut oil, plus more for greasing

½ cup (120 ml) pure maple syrup

½ cup (120 ml) rose water

1½ cups (114 g) unsweetened coconut flakes

Preheat the oven to 350°F (177°C).

In a large mixing bowl, whisk together the buckwheat groats, oats, pepitas, sunflower seeds, flaxseeds, flax meal and salt.

In a food processor or blender, purée the beets, melted coconut oil, maple syrup and rose water until smooth. The beet mixture should yield approximately 2 cups (421 g). Pour the beet mixture over the dry ingredients, and stir to combine.

Grease a 9 x 13–inch (23 x 33–cm) sheet pan with the coconut oil. Spread the beet mixture evenly over the pan.

Bake for 20 minutes, then shake, add the coconut flakes and spread into an even layer. Return to the oven and bake for 15 to 20 minutes until crisp.

Remove from the heat, and transfer to a cooling rack. Once cooled, transfer the granola to an airtight container.

Serve with milk, and enjoy the rosy hue that emerges!

TIPS & TRICKS
Dark sweet cherries complement the flavor and color of this granola. Add them right before serving.

Lemon-Lavender Granola

Buckwheat Groats, Rolled Oats | **Makes 8 cups (1.3 kg)**

I once spent a very relaxing semester in Aix-en-Provence, France, happily immersed in the slower pace of provincial life. It was my intro to the French language, the beginning of my love affair with cheese and the first time I considered lavender to be an ingredient. What amber waves of grain are to America, purple fields of lavender are to Provence. This granola is an everyday opportunity to plot, scheme and dream about a lavender season trip to Provence while savoring the last sips of lavender infused milk.

Grinding the lavender infuses a light floral taste without chomping on floral buds. To find "edible," "culinary" or "food grade" and, ideally, *organic* lavender, try your local co-op bulk spice/teas or check online. These qualifiers should mean the lavender hasn't been treated with pesticides, but opt for organic for extra assurance. Rolled oats are a traditional granola ingredient, but the buckwheat groats are a textural game changer. They are a rich source of rutin, a powerful antioxidant that helps prevent cell damage and supports good health, so this granola will leave you glowing like a French girl.

1 cup (22 g) culinary lavender
1½ cups (255 g) hulled buckwheat groats
1½ cups (120 g) rolled oats
½ cup (80 g) flaxseeds
¼ cup (43 g) flaxseed meal
1 cup (120 g) walnuts
1 tsp (5 g) sea salt
½ cup (120 ml) melted coconut oil, plus more for greasing
½ cup (120 ml) honey
Zest and juice of 2 lemons
1 tsp (5 ml) vanilla extract

Preheat the oven to 350°F (177°C).

In a spice or coffee grinder, grind the lavender buds into a powder. Add to a large mixing bowl with the buckwheat groats, rolled oats, flaxseeds, flaxseed meal, walnuts and salt.

Combine the melted coconut oil, honey, lemon zest, lemon juice and vanilla in a graduated measuring cup or small bowl. If the honey isn't dissolving, heat the liquid ingredients in a saucepan over low heat until combined. Pour the liquid mixture over the dry ingredients, and stir to combine.

Grease a 9 x 13–inch (23 x 33–cm) sheet pan with coconut oil. Spread the mixture evenly over the pan. Clumping is okay (it makes for some cookie-like bites as a bonus!)

Bake for 15 minutes, then turn, and bake another 10 to 15 minutes, until golden. It's best to err on the side of under baking with this mix because the slightest burn will overpower the delicate floral flavor.

Remove from the heat, and transfer to a cooling rack. Once cooled, transfer to an airtight container. Serve with milk or over yogurt, and top with fresh fruit like blueberries.

Blackberry Matcha Tea Cakes

OAT FLOUR | MAKES 6–8 LARGE MUFFINS/TEA CAKES

These tea cake muffins transport me to the first time I had matcha—just pure, earthy matcha—and hot water. I was at my college mentor's home to share a meal and celebrate the international film festival we had produced. In one semester, Jolanta had empowered me and stretched me in ways I'm still unpacking. She introduced me to global cultures, to issues that never made it to mainstream media and to directors who would later break major stories (we had dinner with Laura Poitras, the director who documented the Edward Snowden story!) Mostly, my mentor exposed me to her own tireless, relentless work ethic. She was and is powerful, and nothing could stand in her way.

The meal was her husband's way of exposing me to another global and cultural outlet: food! At the time, I lived off basic stir-fries, peanut butter and the Whole Foods salad bar when I *really* treated myself (#college). His interest in Asian cuisines and his commitment to shopping at all the ethnic grocery stores was my gateway to matcha before it became a mainstream staple. I sipped that tea so wholeheartedly, perhaps *too* wholeheartedly, unaware of the steep price tag that comes with a concentrated tea.

Now that I know the cost, I use matcha a little more sparingly, but also because a little matcha goes a long way. The matcha in these muffins adds a subtle green hue and a nuttiness that balances the tart and juicy blackberries. These muffins will disappear before your tastebuds can pinpoint the source of that nutty flavor.

2 cups (260 g) oat flour

½ cup (96 g) coconut sugar or raw cane sugar

1 tbsp (7 g) matcha powder

1 tbsp (11 g) baking powder

¼ tsp sea salt

2 eggs

⅓ cup (78 ml) avocado or olive oil

⅔ cup (142 ml) buttermilk

1 tsp almond extract

10 oz (284 g) blackberries

Preheat the oven to 400°F (204°C). Grease the muffin pans and/or line with parchment paper muffin cups, if desired. Set aside.

Sift the flour, sugar, matcha powder, baking powder and salt into a mixing bowl, then whisk gently to combine.

In the bowl of a stand mixer, beat together the eggs, oil, buttermilk and almond extract. Pour the liquid over the dry mixture, and stir to combine.

If your blackberries are really large, cut them into halves or quarters, then fold into the batter; mashing them as you stir is okay. Transfer the batter to the prepared muffin tin, filling each cup about ¾ full.

Bake for 12 to 15 minutes, or until a toothpick inserted in the center of the muffin comes out clean. Transfer to a cooling rack to cool slightly, then serve warm.

> TIPS & TRICKS
> *These muffins are not overly sweet, so go ahead and serve them warm with a slathering of butter and a drizzle of honey or a spread of jam. While you have the matcha out, go ahead and make a warm mug of tea, too.*

Teff Bread Smørrebrød/Smorgasbord

BUCKWHEAT GROATS, TEFF | VEGETARIAN, VEGAN OPTION | MAKES 1 (8 x 4 x 2½–INCH [20 x 10 x 6–CM]) LOAF

If I could return to one era of my life, it would be when my close friend Nina and I lived in the same set of row homes. We'd share morning stoop coffees before heading to work, and in the evenings, we'd go on grand picnic adventures. One of our favorite picnic tricks was to buy the dense, Scandinavian-style bread and make beautiful, wholesome, open-faced sandwiches. Topping the bread felt like an art school exercise, and Nina's creativity and Italian roots pushed my palate in new directions.

Instead of pushing gluten-free bread to be something it (generally) isn't—light and fluffy—this hearty teff bread channels the density. These slices are crunchy, nutty bases for all your favorite toast toppings. Enjoy a new variety morning by morning, or if you have multiple people at your breakfast table, you can create one heck of a healthy sweet and savory spread.

1½ cups (145 g) almond meal
1 cup (130 g) teff flour
3 tbsp (30 g) chia seeds
3 tbsp (5 g) psyllium husk
½ cup (85 g) buckwheat groats
½ cup (80 g) sunflower seeds
2 tsp (7 g) baking powder
½ tsp salt
2 tbsp (30 ml) honey (or maple syrup for vegan option)
2 tbsp (30 ml) apple cider vinegar
2 cups (480 ml) warm water (not boiling)

In a large mixing bowl, combine the almond meal, teff flour, chia seeds, psyllium husk, buckwheat groats, sunflower seeds, baking powder and salt.

In another bowl, whisk together the honey, vinegar and water. Pour the wet mix into the dry mix, and combine thoroughly. The batter will be very wet and grey—not the prettiest—but it will bake into a more golden brown. Cover with a tea towel, and let the dough sit for at least an hour to allow the liquid to be absorbed.

After an hour, preheat the oven to 350°F (177°C). Grease and line a 8 x 4 x 2½–inch (20 x 10 x 6–cm) loaf pan with parchment paper. Transfer the dough to the loaf pan (it will still be a very wet dough). Tap the pan to level it, and smooth the top.

Bake for 60 to 70 minutes. If the top looks too dark, cover with foil and continue to bake. The bread is done when it is dark brown on the surface and firm to the touch in the center.

Transfer the pan to a cooling rack. When the bread is cool to the touch, remove from the pan and continue to cool completely. Once cooled, store in the fridge for up to one week.

THESE ARE SOME OF MY FAVORITE TOPPINGS COMBINATIONS
+ *Goat cheese, blueberries and rosemary*
+ *Mascarpone cheese, red grapes, hazelnuts and fresh dill*
+ *Peanut butter, honey and bananas (try it with a dash of cinnamon and nutmeg too!)*
+ *Cream cheese, lox, capers and dill*
+ *Cream cheese, cucumbers and dill*
+ *Jam and fresh berries*
+ *Cream cheese and avocado (maybe some hot sauce too)*

Griddled Golden Raisin Bread

Teff Flour | Vegetarian | Makes 1 (8 x 4 x 2½–inch [20 x 10 x 6–cm]) loaf

I lived in France for almost a year, first as a student in Provence and then as a *jeune fille au pair* (nanny) in Paris, but the title that fit me best (albeit a self-proclaimed title)? Professional picnicker. My budget was always small, but trips to the farmers' markets produced feasts.

The spreads were lessons in regional traditions and filled me with awe for the purveyors. Those "pique-nique" views were hard to beat too. Whether I was staring at the mountains Cézanne painted in the South, or the banks of the Seine, the landscapes were so storied. I miss so many elements of my life there. I miss the bustle and wonder of Paris and from Provence? Oh, how I miss the bread!

Filled with nuts and fruits or savory olives and herbs, the traditional breads were so hearty and wholesome. This breakfast loaf is my way of transporting you to Provence. It's chock full of dried fruits, nuts and seeds with a hint of pumpkin and herbs. Enjoy it with Bonne Maman jam for the true French experience, or try it griddled. Topped with a drizzle (or three!) of pure maple syrup and a dollop of homemade whipped cream, this bread tastes like French toast. It's a bit indulgent, but if there's one thing I learned in France, it's that food should be a celebration, and your breakfast is no exception.

Golden Raisin Bread

½ cup (85 g) raw almonds
½ cup (60 g) raw pecans
¼ cup (85 g) raw pumpkin seeds
½ cup (76 g) golden raisins
½ cup (76 g) prunes, chopped
2 tbsp (20 g) sesame seeds
2 tbsp (20 g) golden flaxseeds
1 cup (130 g) teff flour
1½ tbsp (4 g) fresh rosemary, chopped
2 tsp (5 g) pumpkin pie spice
1 tsp baking soda
1 tsp salt
1 cup (240 ml) buttermilk
1 cup (180 g) pumpkin purée
¼ cup (60 ml) maple syrup
4 eggs

To Serve

1 tbsp (15 ml) unsalted butter
Maple syrup
Homemade whipped cream

TIPS & TRICKS
Double the batch, bake two loaves and stick one loaf in the freezer. Then you're ready to make the Golden Raisin Crackers on page 133, so go ahead and start planning a cheese-centric picnic.

To make the bread, preheat the oven to 350°F (177°C). Grease and line a 8 x 4 x 2½–inch (20 x 10 x 6–cm) loaf pan with parchment paper and set aside.

Spread the almonds, pecans and pumpkin seeds on a sheet pan, and toast for 7 to 10 minutes, tossing them and keeping an eye on them to prevent them from burning. It helps to keep them in separate rows, so you can remove a nut or seed easily if it starts to brown faster. Remove from the oven and transfer to a cutting board. Let them cool to the touch, then chop the nuts coarsely with a knife.

In a mixing bowl, combine the chopped nuts and pumpkin seeds with raisins, chopped prunes, sesame seeds and flaxseeds.

In a large bowl, whisk together the teff flour, rosemary, pumpkin pie spice, baking soda and salt.

In the bowl of a stand mixer, beat the buttermilk, pumpkin purée, maple syrup and eggs. Stir the dry mixture into the wet mixture, then fold in the nut-seed mixture.

Pour the batter into the loaf pan. Bake for 60 to 70 minutes, until the top is firm, and a toothpick inserted in the center comes out clean. If the top starts to brown too early, cover with foil, then continue to bake. With gluten-free breads, you tend to have to bake them longer than expected, but it's best to err on the side of over baking a bit, so the inside won't be mushy (been there/done that!). Transfer to a cooling rack, and let the bread come to room temperature.

To serve, heat the butter in a skillet over medium heat. Add a slice of bread and heat until golden brown around the edges, about 1 to 2 minutes, flip and repeat. Serve with pure maple syrup and a dollop of whipped cream.

Brûléed Grapefruit with Popped Amaranth

AMARANTH | VEGAN OPTION | MAKES 2 SERVINGS

For one spring break trip, I exchanged the dreary cold of Pittsburgh for the warmth of Phoenix, Arizona, to visit my aunt (and her pug!). As I walked her neighborhood, soaking up the desert sun, I couldn't help but fixate on the number of grapefruits spilling from the trees, piling in the yards, along fences and tumbling over curbs. With one bite from a fruit picked fresh from her own tree, I *finally* understood grapefruit. That bite was so much sweeter than the bitter grapefruits I had eaten in Pennsylvania. If you, like me, don't live in a climate with the option for fresh-picked grapefruit bursting with natural sweetness, brûléeing is the next best option. The popped amaranth is not only a super fun process and adorable—think tiny, tiny popcorn—but it adds a wholesome little crunch.

Popped Amaranth
1–2 tbsp (11–22 g) amaranth

Brûléed Grapefruit
1 grapefruit, cut in half crosswise
½–1 tsp (2–4 g) coconut sugar or brown sugar

To Serve
Greek yogurt or nondairy alternative

To make the popped amaranth, you'll need a small saucepan with a lid, so you don't end up with tiny grains everywhere. Heat the pan over medium-high heat. A hot pan is the key to getting the grains to pop. If they burn, it means the pan wasn't hot enough, so test a few grains at a time to make sure you have the temperature right. Then, add the amaranth, and it should begin to pop within seconds of hitting the heat. Cover with a glass lid (for visibility), swirl the pan briefly for even exposure and remove from heat once the majority of the amaranth is popped. Transfer to a small dish and set aside.

To make the brûléed grapefruit, preheat a broiler. If your grapefruits are wobbly, cut a thin slice off the bottom of each half, so that it will stand upright. Use a serrated knife to loosen the segments from the peel. Place the halves upright in a baking dish. Sprinkle the coconut sugar over the grapefruit, and place under the broiler, until the sugar is evenly bubbly and caramelized, 2 to 3 minutes.

To serve, transfer each grapefruit half to an individual dish, top with Greek yogurt and a sprinkle of popped amaranth.

Iced Oat-Milk Lattes with Honey Simple Syrup

STEEL-CUT OATS | MAKES 4 CUPS (946 ML) OAT MILK, ABOUT ¾ CUP (177 ML) HONEY SYRUP

This is an economical trick to have up your sleeve if you want to offer a dairy-free alternative to guests or to toss up your milk routines. Homemade oat milk is a healthier alternative to store-bought, in that it forgoes the stabilizers and fillers—it's just two simple ingredients! You can use rolled oats, but I found the flavor to be a little grassier versus the nuttier flavor and texture of steel-cut oats. Once you have the basic ratios down, you'll be making this in your sleep.

The lightness of this oat milk offers a balance to a hearty, filling granola or you can take a cue from the growing coffee shop trends, and use oat milk with your cold brew in the summer months. For a more indulgent iced latte, try the honey simple syrups for a hint of sweetness with the added health benefits of honey.

Steel-Cut Oat Milk

1 cup (161 g) steel-cut oats
4 cups (946 ml) filtered water

Honey Simple Syrup

1 cup (240 ml) honey
1 cup (240 ml) filtered water

Lavender Flavor Infusion

Peel from 1 lemon
3 tbsp (2 g) dried food-grade lavender
1 vanilla bean, split in half

Rose Flavor Infusion

1 vanilla bean, split in half
¼ cup (7 g) dried food-grade rose petals
¼ cup (23 g) whole cardamom pods, crushed

Iced Latte

6 oz (170 ml) cold brew concentrate
6 oz (170 ml) oat milk
1–2 tbsp (15–30 ml) honey simple syrup

To make the oat milk, combine the oats and water, and soak overnight, or until the oats absorb the liquid and soften. After soaking, pulse the mixture in a blender, just until oats are pulverized, and the mixture is creamy. Be careful not to overblend, or the oat milk can become slimy. Transfer the mixture to cheesecloth draped over a fine-mesh strainer, and strain until liquids are separated from pulpy solids. The resulting liquid is your oat milk. Store in an airtight jar in the fridge for up to about 5 days.

To make the honey syrup, combine the water and honey in a small saucepan. Bring to a boil over medium-high, stirring until the honey dissolves, about 1 to 2 minutes. Remove from the heat, add flavor infusions and cool to room temperature. For a stronger flavor, leave the flavor infusions in overnight. Strain and store in an airtight container in the refrigerator.

To make one iced latte, combine the cold brew concentrate, oat milk and a tablespoon or two (15 or 30 ml) of the flavored honey simple syrup over ice.

TIPS & TRICKS

For a creamier milk, use less water and don't waste that remaining oat pulp. Use the pulp to make a hot breakfast porridge, add it to a smoothie or fold it into a waffle batter.

Brunch

Sweet & Savory Salvation

Ah brunch, society's way of justifying lazing about, eating too much, doing very little and marrying sweet, savory and *saucy*. . . . Pop that champagne!

Hosting brunches has been my salvation. Years ago, I found myself stuck in a job that had me living for Sundays, when I would invite friends into my dining room. I'd encourage them to bring a friend I didn't know, and over French presses and pancakes, the world would become all the smaller.

Planning the menu, setting the table, arranging flowers and serving beautiful, nourishing meals were the seeds that blossomed into my styling career. I eventually found the courage to leave the job I hated, but brunch is *still* sacred, perhaps even *more* sacred because of the way sharing my home and my table has shaped me. Never underestimate what can blossom from slowing down and engaging over brunch.

As a hostess, I feel a responsibility to offer a memorable experience and to serve food my guests can feel good about. That means sourcing the best quality ingredients. That means adding *just* enough sweetness through ingredients like honey, maple syrup or raw cacao. That means stacks of pancakes with iron and calcium-rich teff flour (Big-Batch Multigrain Pancake Mix, page 50). That means sweet and savory flatbreads with amaranth (BYOT [Bring Your Own Toppings] Brunch Flatbreads, page 62), a cholesterol-lowering whole grain. There will be whole grain biscuits loaded with mushroom gravy (Skillet Biscuits & Mushroom Gravy, page 61) and a heap of raw spinach laced with a whole-grain, chocolate-quinoa crunch (A Chocoholic's Brunch Salad, page 66). There will be much to savor, so reach for seconds, and let's settle into the best kind of morning.

Big-Batch Multigrain Pancake Mix

CORNMEAL, SORGHUM FLOUR, TEFF FLOUR | VEGETARIAN | MAKES 4 BATCHES OF PANCAKE MIX,
8–10 (5-INCH [13-CM]) PANCAKES PER BATCH

The lights were shining, the cameras were pointed at me and the producer was giving the countdown—
5, 4, 3, 2, 1 . . . the local news anchor read the monitor without skipping a beat, "We're here in the studio
kitchen with Victoria Bradley, editor-in-chief and stylist Quelcy Kogel of *TABLE* magazine, and we're
talking big-batch pancakes!"

I was nervous and not because I was on live TV. I was nervous because I had to flip a *flippin'* pancake on
live TV! Full disclosure: my journey to a decent pancake flip has been long and tantrum-lined, but there
comes a point in life when you have to face your fears, and for me, it was on the set of KDKA. Flip it I did,
thus propelling my love-hate relationship with pancakes securely to the love side.

If your answer to that weekend question of "What do you want for breakfast?" is, like mine, almost
always pancakes, this big batch of gluten-free pancake mix will put you one step closer to weekend bliss.
The combination of teff, sorghum and cornmeal yields a spongy pancake with enough crunch to absorb
a hearty maple syrup pour.

Big-Batch Multigrain Pancake Mix

2 cups (340 g) cornmeal

2 cups (260 g) sorghum flour

2 cups (260 g) teff flour

2 tsp (8 g) baking powder

2 tsp (9 g) baking soda

1 tsp (5 g) sea salt

Single Batch of Pancakes

1½ cups (195 g) Big-Batch Multigrain
Pancake Mix

1½ cups (355 ml) buttermilk

2 eggs

Butter, for greasing pan

TIPS & TRICKS

*Much like the Go-To Multigrain
Hot Cereal (page 18), a pretty jar
of pancake mix makes a great gift,
especially around the holidays
when families are gathering and
brunch is a must.*

To make the big batch mix, in a large bowl, whisk together the cornmeal, sorghum flour, teff flour, baking powder, baking soda and salt, then transfer to a large resealable plastic bag or glass jar, and store for 6 to 8 weeks. Refrigerate for a longer shelf life (3 to 4 months). Give the mix a good stir before using to integrate any ingredients that may have settled.

To make a single batch of pancakes, add the dry pancake mix to a mixing bowl. In a separate bowl, beat the buttermilk and eggs together. Pour the liquid ingredients over the dry mix, and whisk just enough to combine—some lumps are okay.

Heat a griddle over medium heat. Check to see that the griddle is hot enough by placing a few drops of water onto the griddle. If the water dances across the surface, the griddle is ready. Lightly butter the griddle, then wipe it off thoroughly with a paper towel, so no butter is visible.

Gently ladle the pancake batter onto the griddle. When bubbles begin to set around the edges of the pancake and the griddle-side of the cake is golden, gently flip the pancakes. Continue to cook for 2 to 3 minutes or until the pancake is set.

Serve immediately or transfer to a tea towel–lined baking sheet in a warm oven, and cover with another tea towel. Hold in a warm place until ready to serve, for 20 to 30 minutes maximum.

Fried Pancake Horns

CORNMEAL, SORGHUM FLOUR, TEFF FLOUR │ VEGETARIAN │ MAKES 10 PANCAKE HORNS

"Pancakes for the table," my friend exclaimed, and that moment went down in my personal history as a major turning point. Why had *I*, the queen of halfsies, never thought to order pancakes for the table? Everyone *wants* a pancake at brunch, but they also want to try other menu items. A shared stack of pancakes was the obvious answer.

When you top a pancake with something sweet, fold it like a hand pie, then fry it, you get a sort of hand pie funnel cake fusion. Stuff them with a variety of sweet fillings, dust them with powdered sugar, and you'll take "pancakes for the table" to a whole new level. Think of these as a sweet treat appetizer for your brunch.

1½ cups (195 g) Big-Batch Multigrain Pancake Mix (page 50)

1½ cups (355 ml) buttermilk

2 eggs

Butter, for greasing pan

Filling of your choice

16 oz (453 ml) avocado oil or high heat oil, for frying

Powdered sugar

Add the dry pancake mix to a mixing bowl. In a separate bowl, beat the buttermilk and eggs together. Pour the liquid ingredients over the dry mix, and whisk just enough to combine—some lumps are okay.

Heat a griddle over medium heat. Check to see that the griddle is hot enough by placing a few drops of water onto the griddle. The griddle is ready if the water dances across the surface.

Lightly butter the griddle. Wipe off thoroughly with a paper towel, so no butter is visible.

Pour ¼ cup (60 ml) of batter over the pan, and spread into a thin circle shape. Cook until the batter bubbles, and the surface is relatively dry, about 1 to 2 minutes. Do not flip the pancake! Transfer the unflipped pancake to a pan (uncooked side up), and repeat until all the batter is used. Let the pancakes cool to the touch before filling.

Put a small dollop of filling, about 1 to 2 tablespoons (15 to 30 ml), in the middle of each pancake. Don't overstuff, or the filling will leak. Fold the pancake in half, pressing the edges together to seal.

In a Dutch oven, heat enough oil to cover the pancakes. Heat the oil to 375°F (190°C). Use a slotted spoon to drop the folded pancakes into the oil, and fry until just golden brown, about 40 to 60 seconds per side. Use the slotted spoon to remove, drain the oil and transfer to a paper towel–lined pan.

Serve warm with a dusting of powdered sugar.

THESE ARE SOME OF MY FAVORITE FILLINGS
+   *Lemon curd, ricotta cheese and mashed blueberries*
+   *Homemade Nutella and mashed raspberries*
+   *Mascarpone cheese and jam*
+   *Pumpkin purée, mascarpone cheese, cinnamon and nutmeg*
+   *Dark chocolate ganache*

Multigrain Pancakes with Raspberry-Jalapeño Syrup & Grilled Stone Fruit

CORNMEAL, SORGHUM FLOUR, TEFF FLOUR | MAKES 4 SERVINGS

When I studied abroad in Buenos Aires, my roommates and I would host gatherings for Spanish-speaking exchange students from all over the globe. We'd share drinks, stories and our impressive balcony view of the River soccer stadium. I learned more from those nights than I did in my program.

The Basque students would drink Kalimotxo (cola and red wine), my Peruvian roommate would obsess over *choripan* (Argentine street food sandwich with chorizo) and the Mexican students would roll out their suitcases (!) of spicy snacks and hot sauces. They couldn't leave spice to chance in Argentina—too risky! One of the few items I dared to try was the chili-covered mango, and it opened my eyes to the way a little heat can work in a sweet.

This stack of pancakes would not meet my Mexican roommates' heat standards, but it will change up your pancake routine and surprise your brunch mates. Seeding the jalapeños prevents spice tears but still adds a pleasant warmth. The rum-spiked whipped cream adds a tropical taste that ties the heat, the tart raspberries and the juicy peaches together. Think of these as a vacation in a multigrain stack.

Whipped Cream

1 cup (240 ml) heavy cream, chilled

1 tsp (5 ml) vanilla extract

1 tbsp (15 ml) maple syrup

1–2 tbsp (15–30 ml) spiced rum, to taste, optional

Raspberry-Jalapeño Syrup

10 oz (284 g) raspberries

2 jalapeños, seeded and diced

½ cup (120 ml) honey

Zest and juice of 1 lemon

1 tbsp (15 g) fresh grated ginger

Big Batch Pancakes

1½ cups (195 g) Big-Batch Multigrain Pancake Mix (page 50)

1½ cups (355 ml) buttermilk

2 eggs

Butter, for greasing pan

Grilled Stone Fruit

2 firm peaches or nectarines, halved and pitted

1–2 tbsp (15–30 ml) melted coconut oil

To make the whipped cream, add the heavy cream, vanilla extract and maple syrup to the chilled bowl of a stand mixer. Whisk until the cream reaches soft peaks, then add the rum, if desired, and continue to whisk until stiff peaks form. I tend to go heavy on the rum, so it stands up against the spicy tartness of the syrup. Keep chilled until ready to use.

To make the raspberry-jalapeño syrup, combine all of the ingredients in a medium saucepan and bring to a boil. Reduce to low and simmer until the berries are tender and juicy, and the sauce begins to thicken, approximately 20 minutes. Keep the syrup warm while you make the pancakes.

To make the pancakes, add the dry pancake mix to a mixing bowl. In a separate bowl, beat the buttermilk and eggs together. Pour the liquid ingredients over the dry mix, and whisk just enough to combine—some lumps are okay.

Heat a griddle over medium heat. Check to see that the griddle is hot by placing a few drops of water onto the griddle. The griddle is ready if the water dances across the surface. Lightly butter the griddle. Wipe off thoroughly with a paper towel, so no butter is visible.

Gently ladle the pancake batter onto the griddle. When bubbles begin to set around the edges of the pancake and the griddle-side of the cake is golden, gently flip the pancakes. Continue to cook for 2 to 3 minutes or until the pancake is set. Serve immediately or store in a warm oven until ready to serve.

To make the grilled stone fruit, brush each peach or nectarine half with melted coconut oil, and grill on a grill pan over medium-high heat until tender, about 2 to 3 minutes.

To serve, drizzle a stack of pancakes with the raspberry-jalapeño syrup. Top with a dollop of boozy whipped cream and a grilled peach half.

Cranberry & Goat Cheese–Swirled Sheet Pan Pancake

BUCKWHEAT FLOUR, MILLET FLOUR | MAKES 12 SERVINGS

If I could, I would take you all to the Beaver County Maple Syrup Festival, i.e. my happy place. Once a year, the county's Conservation District hosts this fundraiser and educational program in the park. For more than four decades (!), Boy Scouts and their troop leaders have converted the old barn into a breakfast bonanza, slinging all-you-can-eat buckwheat and buttermilk pancakes and jugs of warm maple syrup tapped from the surrounding trees.

Throw in some Civil War Reenactments, maple syrup demos in the Sugar Shack and vendors selling everything from fresh-milled local flours to fur pelts, and you have something that is so over stimulating and so quintessentially Western Pennsylvania. I can't take everyone there, but a girl can dream and continue to make pancakes in the meantime.

As much as I love eating pancakes, I'm still not the best at flipping them (it's embarrassing). This oven-baked sheet pan pancake eliminates flipping stresses, and instead of feeling like a line cook, you'll be able to join your guests at the table. Everyone can enjoy hot, hearty cakes at the same time. That small victory, my friends, is as near and dear to my heart as the Maple Syrup Festival.

6 tbsp (90 ml) melted butter, divided

2 cups (480 ml) buttermilk

2 large eggs

2 tsp (10 ml) almond extract

1 tsp vanilla extract

1¼ cups (163 g) millet flour

1 cup (130 g) buckwheat flour

2 tsp (8 g) baking powder

1 tsp baking soda

1 tsp kosher salt

¾ cup (181 g) goat cheese, at room temperature

¼ cup (60 ml) whole milk

2 tbsp (17 g) powdered sugar

1 cup (245 g) whole-berry cranberry sauce

Maple syrup, to serve

Preheat the oven to 425°F (220°C). Line an 11 x 17–inch (28 x 43–cm) rimmed baking sheet with parchment paper. Coat the parchment paper and sides of the pan with 2 tablespoons (30 ml) of melted butter. Set aside.

In the bowl of a stand mixer, or with a hand mixer, beat the buttermilk, eggs, almond extract, vanilla and 2 tablespoons (30 ml) of melted butter in a medium bowl until combined.

Sift the the flours, baking powder, baking soda and salt into a separate mixing bowl, and whisk gently to combine. Add the liquid mixture and stir until just combined, do not overmix.

Scrape the batter into the prepared baking sheet, smoothing into an even layer with a spatula.

In the stand mixer, whisk the goat cheese, milk and powdered sugar until completely smooth. Spoon dollops of the goat cheese mixture evenly over the pancake batter. Add dollops of the cranberry sauce, then use a butter knife or a skewer to make a swirl pattern.

Bake until the pancake is lightly golden and springs back in the center when poked, 11 to 13 minutes. Remove from the oven and heat the broiler to high. Brush the remaining 2 tablespoons (30 ml) of melted butter onto the pancake. Broil until golden brown, 1 to 2 minutes, rotating halfway.

Cut into 12 slices, and serve warm with a generous supply of maple syrup.

Cheddar-Jalapeño Waffles
with Oven-"Fried" Chicken

BROWN RICE FLOUR, CORNMEAL, MILLET FLOUR, QUINOA, SORGHUM FLOUR | MAKES 3–4 SERVINGS

There are recipes I develop to prevent myself from going to the same restaurant, for the same dish, on repeat. That's the case with these waffles. I found myself spending way too many Sundays at the same place, but I wasn't the only one. What started as a brunch *special* at the Pittsburgh restaurant Meat & Potatoes became a menu *staple* after so many drool-tinged requests for the infamous Cornmeal Cheddar Jalapeño Waffles with Fried Chicken. How could we not? It's the perfect balance of sweet and savory in one maple drizzled dish.

Once you've tried this oven-"fried" chicken combo, waffle your way through a variety of staple brunch toppings: a short rib hash with a poached egg, smoked fish and quick pickles, breakfast sausages or for vegetarian options, sautéed mushrooms and herbs with a "dippy" egg. For even more variations, play with the heat: drizzle with a hot chili honey or add some hot sauce to your chicken crust for a more Nashville-style tradition—all from the comfort of home. The possibilities are many!

Oven-"Fried" Chicken

See ingredients on page 94 (see also Tips & Tricks)

Cheddar-Jalapeño Waffles

½ cup (65 g) millet flour
½ cup (65 g) sorghum flour
½ cup (85 g) cornmeal
½ tsp baking powder
½ tsp baking soda
¼ tsp sea salt
1½ cups (355 ml) buttermilk
2 eggs
1 tbsp (15 ml) melted coconut oil
1 cup (145 g) raw corn kernels
2 jalapeños, seeded and diced
¾ cup (90 g) shredded cheddar cheese
Crushed black pepper, to taste
Butter, to serve
Maple syrup, to serve

To make the "fried" chicken, prepare the oven-"fried" chicken according to directions on page 94. While the chicken bakes, prepare the waffles.

To make the waffles, preheat a waffle iron according to the manufacturer's instructions.

In a large bowl, whisk the flours, baking powder, baking soda and salt; set aside.

In a small bowl, whisk the buttermilk and eggs. Pour the wet mixture over the flour mixture, and whisk gently to combine. Gently whisk in the coconut oil.

Fold in the corn kernels, jalapeños, cheddar and black pepper.

Following the manufacturer's instructions, cook the waffles until deep brown and crisp. For a standard waffle iron, pour a generous ½ cup (118 ml) of batter into the center, spreading to within ½ inch (1 cm) of the edges, and close; the waffle will cook in 2 to 3 minutes.

Serve warm, with butter, maple syrup and a piece of oven-"fried" chicken.

> TIPS & TRICKS
> *You can skip the pickle brine in the Oven-"Fried" Chicken recipe for a faster process, but the flavor does pair well with the waffles.*

Skillet Biscuits & Mushroom Gravy

MILLET FLOUR, SORGHUM FLOUR | VEGETARIAN | MAKES 4–6 SERVINGS

When the Ace Hotel first opened in Pittsburgh, I had the privilege of attending a soft opening brunch at its restaurant, Whitfield, but there was *nothing* soft about that brunch. Clearly having missed their construction deadlines, projects were still very much in the works. That brunch was eye opening, not only because we had to keep an eye out for danger, but because that was the brunch that introduced me to mushroom gravy!

Leave your rolling pin in the drawer because these drop biscuits are not fussy. Whole grain sorghum and millet add a little extra density, but they also add a savory, buttery flavor. The vegan mushroom gravy will win over meat eaters and plant eaters alike, and to really live your best brunch life, top the combo with a poached or "dippy" egg. For my fellow sweet *teeth* out there, these biscuits also pair well with butter and jam.

Biscuits

1–2 tbsp (15–30 ml) melted butter or oil, for greasing

1½ cups (195 g) sorghum flour

1 cup (130 g) millet flour

4 tsp (15 g) baking powder

1½ tsp (6 g) ground psyllium husk powder

1 tsp salt

5 tbsp (72 g) chilled butter, divided

⅔ cup (155 ml) buttermilk

2 eggs

Gravy

½ cup (120 ml) avocado oil

½ cup (75 g) small onion, finely chopped

1 cup (75 g) chopped baby portobello mushrooms

½ cup (65 g) millet flour

3 cups (720 ml) vegetable stock

1 tsp Bragg's amino acids or gluten-free soy sauce

½ tsp sea salt

¼ tsp black pepper

Fresh herbs such as thyme and rosemary, to serve

> ### TIPS & TRICKS
> *Keep this gravy recipe in your arsenal for entertaining vegans. Its meaty flavor works well as a sauce. For vegetarians, poached or "dippy" eggs will take the biscuit and gravy combo to the next level and bring friends back weekly for encores.*

To make the biscuits, preheat the oven to 425°F (220°C). Lightly grease a skillet with oil or melted butter, and set it aside. Sift the sorghum flour, millet flour, baking powder, ground psyllium husk powder and salt into a medium-size mixing bowl. Whisk gently to combine the ingredients.

Use your fingers or a pastry cutter to cut 4 tablespoons (58 g) of butter into the flour mixture, until the butter is the size of small peas. Some flatter pieces of butter are okay too.

In a graduated measuring glass or a separate mixing bowl, whisk the buttermilk and egg together until frothy.

Create a well in the middle of the dry ingredients, and pour the liquid into the center. Use a spatula to mix, and stir until evenly moistened. Scoop a heaping tablespoon (15 ml) from the batter and gently form into a ball. Place in the skillet and repeat, leaving a little space between biscuits. You should have 12 biscuits total.

Bake for 12 to 15 minutes until the biscuits are golden and the tops are firm. Melt the remaining tablespoon (14 g) of butter and brush over the tops of the biscuits for the last 1 to 2 minutes of baking. While the biscuits bake, prepare the gravy.

To make the gravy, in a large skillet, heat the oil over medium-high heat. Add the onion and mushrooms; cook, stirring, until well browned, 8 to 10 minutes. Sprinkle in the flour and cook, stirring, until golden brown, 3 to 5 minutes.

Slowly whisk in the vegetable stock, a little at a time, until a smooth sauce forms. If you want a thinner consistency of gravy, you can add another cup (240 ml) of vegetable broth. Simmer 2 to 3 minutes until thickened.

Reduce the heat to low, add the amino acids, salt and pepper, then add your herbs. This is a great recipe for cleaning out the lingering herbs in your fridge. I recommend thyme or rosemary, but oregano, chives or tarragon would also work. Serve chunky, or combine in a food processor for a smoother consistency.

Serve everything warm with additional fresh herbs for garnish.

BYOT (Bring Your Own Toppings) Brunch Flatbreads

AMARANTH | VEGETARIAN OPTIONS | MAKES 1 FLATBREAD, ABOUT 3–6 SERVINGS

I began experimenting with gluten-free baking options to host more inclusive gatherings, but there's also something to be said for the challenge of eliminating gluten. This flatbread is a lesson in restriction and magic—much like an episode of *Iron Chef*. The process feels like alchemy—tiny amaranth grains soaked in water overnight, blended with a few ingredients and baked—become a carrier for your favorite sweet and savory combinations.

It's definitely *not* a pizza (I'm *very* careful not to encourage pizza expectations to gluten-free eaters—that's just mean). It *is* like a spongy, seedy, hearty pita, and it works so well for brunch. Just set those grains to soak Friday night, and by Saturday morning, you'll be toasting champagne and passing slices.

1 cup (161 g) uncooked amaranth

½ cup (120 ml) water

3 tbsp (45 ml) apple cider vinegar

1 tbsp (15 g) nutritional yeast

½ tsp baking powder

½ tsp salt

½ tsp garlic powder

½ tsp ground thyme

Avocado oil, for greasing

Toppings of your choice

Soak the amaranth in water, covering it by at least 1 inch (2.5 cm). Let the amaranth soak overnight (or for at least 8 hours).

After the amaranth has soaked, preheat the oven to 425°F (220°C).

Rinse the amaranth in a fine strainer, then transfer to a blender or a food processor with ½ cup (120 ml) of water. Add the remaining ingredients, except the oil and toppings, and blend until the mixture is a creamy liquid.

Line a 9 x 13–inch (23 x 33–cm) baking dish with parchment paper and grease lightly with avocado oil. Pour the crust batter into the pan and use a spatula to evenly distribute the batter.

Bake the crust for 18 minutes on one side. Carefully flip the crust, and cook for an additional 15 minutes until the crust is golden and crispy.

Top the flatbread with your toppings of choice, and return to the oven for an additional 5 to 8 minutes. Remove from the oven, slice and serve.

TIPS & TRICKS

Kill two birds with one stone and serve with the A Chocoholic's Brunch Salad (page 66). Double the roasted strawberries and serve some as flatbread toppers. Make your brunch party more interactive and have friends bring their favorite flatbread toppings. Have the flatbreads baked and ready to assemble. You could even make smaller flatbreads, so friends can make their own individual servings.

THESE ARE SOME OF MY FAVORITE FLAVOR PAIRINGS

+ *Ricotta cheese, pesto, grilled asparagus, grilled sweet corn, shaved and grated Parmesan*
+ *Ricotta cheese, bacon, roasted portobello or chanterelle mushrooms, kale and shaved Parmesan*
+ **Mascarpone cheese, roasted strawberries, blueberries, balsamic reduction and mint*
+ **Ricotta cheese, grilled peaches or nectarines, blueberries, slivered almonds, balsamic reduction and fresh thyme*

*For these variations, skip the garlic powder and ground thyme from the recipe, and experiment with other "sweet" spices like cinnamon or ginger.

Heirloom Tomato Tart

BROWN RICE FLOUR, TEFF FLOUR | VEGETARIAN | MAKES 1 (10-INCH [25-CM]) TART, ABOUT 8 SERVINGS

If teachers, aunts, uncles and even parents can (and do) have favorite kids (I'm obviously the favorite), then farmers can most certainly have a favorite fruit of their labors. For my fella, I would put my money on the gallon jug of deep amber honey, hard-earned through swollen hands and cheeks after suffering the consequences of riled bees. For yours truly, a meager farmhand and observer, it's the juicy, bulbous tomatoes.

The sweet juiciness of summer tomatoes is instant gratification on long, hot days and a reminder of living in the moment. The sad winter counterparts, hardly even a distant relative of summer's gorgeous heirlooms, will never, ever be as fulfilling, nor should they be. This tart is an ode to heirloom tomatoes when they're at their sweetest and juiciest, and that's cause for celebration, so invite some friends to share in the peak of the season.

Tart Crust

1 cup (151 g) brown rice flour

¼ cup (32 g) teff flour

¼ cup (31 g) arrowroot starch/powder/ flour

½ tsp whole psyllium husk

½ tsp ground thyme

½ tsp garlic powder

½ tsp salt

1 stick unsalted butter, chilled and cut into six pieces, plus more for greasing

¼ cup (60 ml) apple cider vinegar, chilled

Tart Filling

1 cup (123 g) ricotta cheese

½ cup (90 g) grated Parmesan or pecorino cheese

⅓ cup (14 g) chopped basil

Juice and zest of 1 lemon

Fresh crushed black pepper, to taste

1–2 heirloom tomatoes, sliced ¼ inch (6 mm) thick

To Serve

Grated Parmesan or pecorino

Fresh herbs like thyme or basil

Basil Vinaigrette (page 102)

To make the crust, lightly grease a 9- or 10-inch (23- or 25-cm) tart pan with butter. In the bowl of food processor, combine brown rice flour, teff flour, arrowroot starch, psyllium husk, ground thyme, garlic powder and salt. Pulse to combine then add the butter. Pulse until no large pieces remain. Add the apple cider vinegar, and run the food processor until a dough forms. If you don't like the acidic punch of apple cider vinegar, you can use chilled water. Use your fingers to press the dough into the tart pan. Use a fork to prick the bottom dough to prevent bubbling during baking. Freeze the tart crust for 30 minutes. Meanwhile, prepare the filling.

To make the filling, in a mixing bowl, stir together the ricotta, Parmesan, chopped basil, lemon juice, lemon zest and black pepper.

Position a rack in the lower third of the oven and preheat to 400°F (204°C). Place the chilled tart pan on a baking sheet. Cover the dough with a piece of parchment paper and fill the pan with pie weights (or dried beans will work) to prevent the dough from bubbling or sliding off the sides. Bake for 12 minutes, then carefully remove the weights and parchment paper, and continue baking until the crust is light golden brown, about 10 minutes. Transfer to a wire rack and add the ricotta mixture. Top with the tomato slices. Cool completely before serving. While the tart cools, prepare the vinaigrette (page 102).

If your tomatoes are a little lackluster, you can enhance the sweetness a bit by returning the tart to the oven for 3 to 5 minutes after adding the filling. The cheese mixture and tomatoes will release a lot of juices, but the liquids will settle again, or you can speed up the process and dab them with a paper towel.

Sprinkle the tart with cheese and fresh herbs and a drizzle of basil vinaigrette to serve.

A Chocoholic's Brunch Salad

QUINOA | MAKES 4–6 SERVINGS

Two chocoholics walk into a plant conservatory. No, it's not the setup of a joke, it's the beginning of one of my fonder food memories. More than a decade ago, Pittsburgh's Phipp's Conservatory featured a show simply called "Chocolate!" There were chocolate fountains and even chocolate flamingos in a garden (!), but my sister Tonya and I went straight for the chocolate-themed menu. When we saw the words "chocolate" and "salad" *together*, we found a happy place I've been longing to recreate for years.

Salads often fail to attract the attention pancakes and frittatas monopolize at brunch, but serve this, and friends will go back for thirds. The raw cacao adds the sweet-tooth-satisfying chocolate flavor you crave, but you're eating high-protein, crunchy quinoa and a heap of greens. The wine-roasted strawberries are indulgent, but that's why this is a *brunch* salad. This recipe is best served DIY style, so simply place all the components on the table, and let your fellow brunchers dive in and enjoy.

Chocolate-Quinoa Crunchers (page 33)

Roasted Strawberries

2 tbsp (30 ml) honey

1 tbsp (15 g) coconut oil

1 lb (454 g) strawberries

1 tbsp (15 ml) Grand Marnier or port wine

1 tsp pomegranate or balsamic vinegar

¼ tsp sea salt

Dash of fresh ground black pepper

Chocolate Citrus Vinaigrette

1 orange

2 tbsp (23 g) raw cacao

¼ cup (60 ml) olive oil

¼ cup (60 ml) pomegranate vinegar or balsamic

1 tsp honey

½ tsp sea salt

⅛ tsp black pepper

To Serve

Spinach

Arugula

Mint

Bleu cheese

To make the Chocolate Quinoa Crunchers, prepare the quinoa as directed on page 33, and set aside.

To make the strawberries, preheat the oven to 350°F (177°C). In a saucepan over medium heat, melt the honey and coconut oil together until just combined, then transfer to a mixing bowl. Wash, hull and slice the strawberries, reserving the tops. Add the strawberries, liquer, vinegar, salt and pepper to the mixing bowl. Stir gently to coat the strawberries in the liquid, then set aside to marinate for 20 minutes. After the strawberries have marinated, transfer the strawberries and the liquid to a parchment paper–lined sheet tray. Roast for 20 minutes. The strawberries should keep their shape, but they'll soften and start to caramelize. While the strawberries are roasting, make the dressing.

To make the dressing, juice and zest the orange into a glass jar. Add the raw cacao, oil, vinegar, honey, salt and pepper. Seal the lid and give it a good shake. Store in the refrigerator until ready to use.

Remove the strawberries from the oven and set aside to cool to room temperature. The syrup will thicken slightly. Serve the strawberries with their liquid at room temperature. If the coconut oil starts to solidify, warm it in a saucepan.

Spoon the strawberries over fresh greens and mint to serve. Top with Chocolate-Quinoa Crunchers and bleu cheese crumbles.

> TIPS & TRICKS
> *Add those washed strawberry tops to a pitcher of water for a pretty and refreshing, strawberry flavored beverage. You'll waste less, and the flavored water helps balance the adult brunch beverages.*

Savory Oats with Maple Sausage & Cherry Sauce

STEEL-CUT OATS | MAKES 4 SERVINGS

High protein, whole-grain steel-cut oats are whole oat groats cut into little pieces on a steel mill, hence the name. Often toasted, they yield a chewier, full-bodied hot cereal with a little more nuance than their rolled oat counterpart. The price for that extra flavor and texture, however, is time, which is why I reserve steel-cut oats for weekends. Oatmeal might not seem like it'd merit a spot at a brunch gathering, but when paired with maple breakfast sausage and saucy cherries, it's a dish worthy of the spotlight, especially during the months when everyone wants to hibernate.

Savory Oatmeal

3 cups (709 ml) vegetable broth
1 cup (240 ml) water, optional
1 cup (161 g) steel-cut oats
Sea salt and freshly ground pepper, to taste
2 tbsp (30 g) unsalted butter
¼ cup (45 g) grated Parmesan
1 cup (245 g) Greek yogurt
2 tbsp (30 ml) maple syrup

Sausage and Cherries

3 tbsp (45 g) unsalted butter, divided
1 medium yellow onion, chopped
6 (about 14 oz [397 g]) maple pork breakfast sausage links
1 cup (152 g) cherries, pitted
2 tbsp (30 ml) maple syrup, plus more to taste
1 cup (240 ml) fruity red wine
2 tbsp (30 ml) red wine vinegar
Kosher salt
Freshly ground pepper, to taste
2 sprigs thyme
Zest of 1 orange

Maple-Toasted Walnuts

1 cup (116 g) walnut halves
3 tbsp (45 ml) maple syrup
Pinch of salt

Maple syrup, for serving

To make the oats, pour the broth into a large saucepan over medium-high heat. For a firmer, grainier textured oatmeal, use only the broth. If you want a creamier oatmeal, add 1 cup (240 ml) of water as well. Bring the liquid to a boil. Stir in the oats, salt and pepper, and bring to a roiling boil, it only takes a few seconds, being careful to avoid foaming and overflowing.

Once boiling, reduce the heat to low, and bring the oats to a low simmer. Let the oats simmer anywhere from 20 to 30 minutes, stirring occasionally and scraping the bottom of the pan to prevent sticking. Cook until the oats are tender and have reached your desired creaminess—the longer you cook it, the creamier the consistency. Whisk in the butter and grated Parmesan. Remove from the heat, stir in the Greek yogurt and maple syrup. Cover and keep warm until ready to serve.

While the oats are simmering, prepare the sausage. Heat 2 tablespoons (30 g) of butter in a large saucepan over medium heat until melted and sizzling. Add the chopped onion, and continue to cook, stirring until the onion is soft and translucent, about 5 minutes. Reduce the heat to medium-low, and continue to cook until the onion is amber-colored, 15 to 20 minutes.

Slice the sausages, add them to the pan and cook for 6 to 8 minutes, until browned and partially cooked. Add the cherries, crushing some with a spoon as you stir. Cook, until the sausages are cooked through and the cherries are slightly saucy, about 5 minutes. Drizzle in the maple syrup, and cook for 1 more minute, stirring frequently. Transfer the sausages and cherries to a plate, but leave any liquid in the pan.

Add the red wine and vinegar to the pan, and cook until thickened and syrupy, about 5 minutes. Remove from the heat and add 1 tablespoon (15 g) of butter, swirling the pan to incorporate the butter into the sauce. Return the sausage and cherries to the saucepan. Season with salt and pepper. Remove the thyme from the sprigs, and sprinkle the thyme leaves and orange zest over the mixture. Keep warm while you toast the walnuts.

To make the walnuts, preheat a dry skillet over medium-high heat. Add the walnuts, maple syrup and salt. Cook, stirring frequently, until the syrup is caramelized and nuts are toasted, about 3 minutes. Let cool slightly, then transfer to a cutting board and roughly chop with a knife.

To serve, divide the oatmeal among bowls. Top with the sausage and cherries, and drizzle with extra sauce. Garnish with the maple-toasted walnuts and a drizzle of maple syrup.

Grain
Bowls

A Bowl, A Pan & A Meal Prepping Plan

More substantial than a salad, yet equally imprecise, the beauty of the grain bowl is its looseness. You are your own guru when it comes to the grain bowl. Trust your instincts. Unlike baking, forgetting an ingredient or overdoing another will not make or break the outcome. Clean out your fridge. Sauce it up. You don't *need* me, but I still wanted to give you some inspiration on the bowl front. I'm offering you this meal prep formula: grains + sheet pan + sauce. Think of this section as creating dishes to share with yourself. You might also want to share the recipes with your coworkers, who will be *grain* with envy.

Some General Grain Bowl Tips & Tricks

Pick Your Grains. Millet, quinoa, rice and sorghum tend to work the best in grain bowls because their textures are more pronounced. Amaranth, cornmeal, oats and teff yield creamier, porridge-like textures, which can be delicious bases for savory dishes, but they don't yield that satisfying grain bowl crunch. Buckwheat groats, when prepared al dente, hold up well too, but their flavor is earthier and stronger. I recommend mixing buckwheat with another grain such as quinoa, until you're more accustomed to its flavor.

Mix Your Grains. The grains listed in these recipes are suggested pairings. If you return to these combinations again and again, experiment with different grains. There's no rule saying you have to stick to just one grain either. Many of the textures are complementary. For example, adding the larger sorghum "pearls" to quinoa can make for a more varied bite.

Embellish Your Grains. Don't just cook those grains with water. Substituting a low-sodium stock, a portion of citrus juice or apple cider vinegar intensifies the savory flavors of the grains. Additionally, you can add a tea bag to the liquid while cooking. The earthy flavors of green tea work well and add antioxidants. Be sure to use organic teas though, since teas are never washed (because washing would effectively be making the tea). Any pesticides used in farming linger in the tea leaves, and that's the last ingredient I'd want you to be eating in a bowl.

The Lili Bowl: Pistachio- & Cashew-Crusted Salmon with Carrot-Ginger Dressing

WILD RICE OR BROWN RICE | MAKES 4 SERVINGS

Lili was my neighborhood coffee shop/cafe. Not only was it conveniently close (I could easily stumble there in a pre-coffee stupor), but Heidi, the owner, created a really innovative menu from a very minimal kitchen. (We're talking hot plates here!) Lili was slinging grain bowls before every magazine and food website had "10 Ways to Make the Best Bowl" articles. Their classic kimchi bowl combined brown rice, fresh greens, avocado, hard-boiled egg and an optional lox upgrade, which I always chose. The real distinguishing factor was the bright orange carrot-ginger dressing.

Lili has since switched hands to become Kaibur, but by popular demand, the grain bowl lives on. Since I have a kitchen with more resources, my ode to the Lili bowl includes a lox upgrade to a pistachio- and cashew-crusted salmon. Remember to drizzle the dressing generously because that's the Lili legacy.

Pistachio- & Cashew-Crusted Salmon Sheet Pan

4 (approximately 4–6 oz [113–170 g] each) wild-caught skin on salmon fillets (wild King or your favorite variety)

1 bunch broccoli, cut into florets

4 baby bok choy, cut in half lengthwise

2 shallots, cut in halves

Zest and juice of 1 lemon

2 tbsp (30 ml) coarse-grain or Dijon mustard

2 tbsp (30 ml) honey

¼ cup (30 g) shelled pistachios

¼ cup (30 g) unsalted, roasted cashews

2 tbsp (17 g) teff flour

1 tbsp (15 ml) avocado oil

1 tbsp (15 ml) sesame oil

Salt and pepper, to taste

Carrot-Ginger Dressing

¼ cup (38 g) chopped shallots (or the roasted shallots from the sheet pan)

½ lb (227 g) carrots (3 medium), coarsely chopped

¼ cup (58 g) chopped peeled fresh ginger

¼ cup (60 ml) rice vinegar

Juice of 1 lemon

1 tbsp (15 ml) Bragg's amino acids or gluten-free soy sauce

Salt, to taste

1 tbsp (15 ml) sesame oil

½ cup (120 ml) avocado oil

¼ cup (60 ml) water

To Serve

4 cups (644 g) cooked wild rice or brown rice

Baby spinach

4 hard-boiled eggs

Avocado

Kimchi

(continued)

The Lili Bowl: Pistachio- & Cashew-Crusted Salmon with Carrot-Ginger Dressing (continued)

To make the salmon, preheat the oven to 375°F (190°C). Line a sheet pan with parchment paper. Rinse the salmon and pat it dry with a paper towel. Arrange the salmon, skin side down, on the sheet pan. Add the broccoli florets, bok choy and shallots to the pan.

In a small bowl, combine the lemon zest, lemon juice, mustard and honey. Spoon the mixture over each salmon fillet and the vegetables.

In a food processor, coarsely chop the pistachios and cashews with teff flour and avocado oil so some larger chunks of nuts remain. Spread the nut mixture over the salmon, pressing lightly to adhere. Drizzle the fish and vegetables with the sesame oil. Season with salt and pepper.

Bake until the salmon is cooked through to your liking and pistachios are golden brown, approximately 15 to 20 minutes. Remove the pan from the oven. Transfer the salmon to a tray or cutting board to rest (the residual heat will continue to cook the salmon slightly, so factor that into your desired "doneness" when you pull the fish from the oven).

If the bok choy is roasted to your liking, remove it from the tray as well. For a really crispy, savory broccoli, return the pan, with the broccoli and shallots, to the oven for another 5 to 10 minutes. Remove from the oven, and set it aside while you prepare the dressing.

To make the dressing, roughly chop the roasted shallots once they are cool enough to handle. Use a food processor or high-speed blender to pulse the chopped shallots and carrots until finely ground (almost puréed). Add the chopped ginger, rice vinegar, lemon juice, aminos and salt, and pulse until the ginger and shallots are minced. With the motor running, add the oils together in a slow stream. Add the water and blend until smooth, 2 to 3 minutes. Thin dressing with additional water, if desired. Store the dressing in an airtight container in the refrigerator.

To serve, combine 1 cup (161 g) of wild or brown rice with a heap of baby spinach, a salmon fillet, bok choy, broccoli, a hard-boiled egg, avocado, kimchi and a drizzle of dressing.

The Meat & Potatoes Bowl

EMPEROR'S RICE | MAKES 4 SERVINGS

My dad raised Piedmontese cows, a particularly muscled breed. He'd position me at a gate and tell me to take up space, to stand my ground, and not let those obstinate, horned beasts pass, but they would test me (and usually win). So entrenched was my dad in the world of cattle that even our Thanksgiving meals frequently featured red meat.

This bowl is for my dad. I wouldn't be *me* without my dad. I wouldn't have big dreams, a head full of ideas and an intense grammar fixation. I wouldn't respect the farmers, growers and animal tenders without seeing his struggles and his passion. If it weren't for him, I wouldn't see neighbors as part of my community or see complete strangers as people who just need a laugh.

This bowl might not look like the middle America meat and potato dishes of my childhood. The steak to vegetables ratio is modest, because the juicy, grilled flank steak is an accent here, complemented by whole roasted mushrooms which add even more meaty flavor. But, this bowl just *might* convince the staunch meat eater in your life to eat some "weird" grains.

Potato Sheet Pan

Avocado oil or high heat oil, for greasing

1 lb (454 g) Brussels sprouts

24 oz (680 g) fingerling potatoes, cut in half, vertically

8 oz (227 g) baby portobello mushrooms

Half a red onion

Flaked sea salt

Fresh cracked pepper

Herbs de Provence

Grilled Steak

½ tsp sea salt

½ tsp crushed black pepper

½ tsp smoked paprika

½ tsp garlic powder

1 (12-oz [340-g]) flank steak

12 oz (340 g) asparagus

Creamy Avocado Bleu Cheese Dressing

1 tbsp (10 g) chopped roasted red onion (from the potato sheet pan)

2 oz (57 g) bleu cheese crumbles

1 avocado

2 tbsp (30 g) Greek yogurt

¼ cup (60 ml) milk or buttermilk

1 tbsp (15 ml) fresh lemon juice or white wine vinegar

1 tsp (5 ml) red wine vinegar

Salt and pepper, to taste

Avocado or olive oil, as needed

To Serve

4 cups (644 g) cooked Emperor's rice

Fresh greens, such as frisee

Avocado slices, optional

Bleu cheese, optional

(continued)

The Meat and Potatoes Bowl (continued)

To make the potato sheet pan, preheat the oven to 375°F (190°C). Grease a 9 x 13–inch (23 x 33–cm) sheet pan with avocado oil. Spread the Brussels sprouts, potatoes, mushrooms and onion evenly over the pan. Drizzle with additional oil and season generously with salt, pepper and herbs de Provence. Saltiness on these veggies will really shine in the finished bowl. Roast the vegetables for 30 to 40 minutes, stirring about halfway through, until the potatoes are browned and crisp.

To make the steak, heat a grill pan over medium-high heat. Combine the salt, pepper, paprika and garlic powder in a small bowl. Pat the spice mixture on both sides of the flank steak, then transfer the steak to the heated grill pan. Grill for 5 minutes on each side for medium-rare, or more for desired doneness. Transfer the meat to a cutting board, but keep the grill pan on medium-high. Let the meat stand for 10 minutes. Meanwhile, grill the asparagus for 10 minutes, flipping periodically, then transfer to the cutting board. Use a long serrated knife to cut the flank steak against the grain and into strips.

To make the dressing, select some thicker onion slices from the roasted vegetables, and chop. Combine the onion, bleu cheese, avocado, Greek yogurt, milk, lemon juice and red wine vinegar in a food processor or blender, and pulse until desired creaminess. Season to taste with salt and pepper. For a thinner consistency, stir in the oil.

To serve, add about 1 cup (161 g) of rice and some fresh greens to a bowl. Top with a mix of roasted vegetables, grilled asparagus and few strips of flank steak. Drizzle with the dressing, and add avocado slices and bleu cheese crumbles, if desired.

The Vegan Gaucho Grain Bowl

EMEPEROR'S RICE │ VEGAN │ MAKES 4–6 SERVINGS

Traveling the Argentine countryside—"Gaucho nation," if you will—I very quickly learned that Argentines have very little reverence for salads. They devote all of their attention to the *asado*, the ritualistic roasting of meat. At the time, I was a student who ate a mostly vegetarian diet, and when I tried to order a salad, the gauchos returned with a few leaves of plain lettuce, so I made peace with the grill and ate the meat. "When in Rome . . . "

Of course, in Buenos Aires, we ate our fair share of contemporary, vegetable-forward dishes, but this bowl is inspired by the smoky, meaty flavors of the countryside, of the traditions of the gaucho. It's an oxymoron with smoky eggplant, meaty mushrooms and a variation on the traditional chimichurri sauce, which you'll want to scoop onto everything.

Roasted Vegetable Sheet Pan

3 tbsp (45 ml) avocado oil, divided

4 (about 8-oz [227-g]) portobello mushroom steaks

1 large eggplant, sliced into rings, then quartered

1 red bell pepper, chopped

1 head of garlic, chopped

1 tsp smoked paprika

Zest of 2 lemons

2–3 sprigs fresh oregano

1 tsp liquid smoke

Salt and pepper, to taste

Chimichurri Sauce

½ cup (120 ml) red wine vinegar

1 tsp sea salt

3–4 cloves garlic, minced

1 shallot, finely chopped

1 jalapeño, seeded and finely chopped

½ cup (20 g) chopped fresh cilantro

½ cup (20 g) chopped fresh flat-leaf parsley

2 tbsp (6 g) finely chopped fresh oregano

2 tsp (7 g) crushed red pepper

1 tbsp (8 g) capers

¾ cup (177 ml) extra virgin olive oil

½ cup (75 g) sun-dried tomatoes, chopped

To Serve

4 cups (644 g) cooked Emperor's rice, black rice or wild rice

Toasted walnuts, chopped

Fresh herbs such as oregano or basil

To make the roasted vegetable sheet pan, preheat the oven to 400°F (204°C). Drizzle a sheet pan with 1 tablespoon (15 ml) of oil. Arrange the vegetables and garlic in an even layer on the pan. Spread the smoked paprika, lemon zest and fresh oregano evenly over the pan.

Combine the remaining oil and liquid smoke in a small bowl, then pour evenly over the tray. Season with salt and pepper to taste. Roast for 25 to 30 minutes, to desired crispness. Meanwhile, prepare the chimichurri so the flavors have time to infuse the oil before serving.

To make the chimichurri, mix all of the ingredients together in a bowl. The crushed red pepper adds a little heat; if you want less spice, decrease or skip it.

To serve, combine the rice, roasted veggies and a heaping spoonful (or two!) of chimichurri in a bowl. Sprinkle with the toasted walnuts, garnish with fresh herbs and enjoy!

> **TIPS & TRICKS**
> *To waste less and glean extra flavor when making the chimichurri, buy sun-dried tomatoes packed in extra virgin olive oil, and use as much of that oil as possible for the sauce.*

Marseille Millet Bowl with Roasted Roots

MILLET | VEGETARIAN, VEGAN OPTION | MAKES 4–6 SERVINGS

Camel was a Moroccan man living in Marseille, France, who happened to be hopelessly in love with my host "mom." He'd join us for dinner, and they'd smoke cigarettes on the balcony, looking cooler than one should when smoking. Camel very graciously offered to show me *his* Marseille, a city I adored for its grit and diversity. Thanks to its immigrant population, Marseille felt like a window into Northern Africa. It had a different pulse than the more traditional French Aix-en-Provence, where I was studying.

Camel led me through bustling city street markets, where bartering for the best dates and figs was a sign of respect. He explained the luck and the nuances behind pouring Moroccan mint tea from shiny tea pots. He also properly introduced me to tagines. Aside from the fall-off-your-fork tender cuts of meat, what surprised me the most was the inclusion of sweet, dried fruits that would plump with the savory juices. This bowl, with golden turmeric, sweet root vegetables, warming, aromatic spices, golden raisins, prunes and the sweet accent of fresh mint, is my tribute to the way Camel shared his heritage and his adopted city with me.

Roasted Root Sheet Pan

2 tbsp (30 g) coconut oil

1 tbsp (15 ml) honey (use maple syrup for vegan option)

1 tsp turmeric

1 tsp ground cumin

3 medium to large golden beets, peeled and quartered

1 bunch radishes, halved

1 lb (454 g) rainbow carrots, peeled and sliced thick

2 lbs (908 g) parsnips, peeled and sliced thick

1½ cups (255 g) (1 can) cooked chickpeas, drained and rinsed

1 cup (151 g) pomegranate seeds

4 cloves garlic, peeled

¼ cup (10 g) finely chopped fresh mint

Millet

1 tbsp (15 g) coconut oil

1 tsp cumin seeds (or ½ tsp ground cumin)

1 cup (185 g) uncooked millet

1 small white or yellow onion, diced

2 stalks celery, trimmed and diced

2½ cups (592 g) low sodium vegetable broth

½ tsp fine salt

1 tsp turmeric

½ tsp coriander

½ tsp ground ginger

¼ tsp cinnamon

½ cup (76 g) golden raisins

½ cup (76 g) prunes, chopped

Roasted Garlic Tahini Dressing

¼ cup (60 ml) olive oil

¼ cup (45 g) tahini

Juice from 1 lemon

¼ tsp sea salt

Black pepper, to taste

Garlic from roasting pans

1–2 tbsp (15–30 ml) water, as needed

To Serve

Chopped kale

Fresh mint

Fresh parsley

Slivered almonds

To make the sheet pan, preheat the oven to 400°F (204°C). Line a sheet pan with parchment paper.

In a saucepan over medium heat, whisk together the coconut oil, honey, turmeric and cumin, until melted. Remove from heat and set aside.

In a large mixing bowl, combine the quartered beets, radish halves, carrot slices, parsnip slices, chickpeas, pomegranate seeds and garlic. Pour the liquid ingredients into the bowl, and toss until evenly coated. Spread the mixture over the sheet pan, top with chopped mint, and roast for 35 to 40 minutes, until the vegetables are tender, tossing halfway through. Meanwhile, prepare the millet.

To make the millet, while the roots roast, heat 1 tablespoon (15 g) of coconut oil in a Dutch oven or stockpot. When the oil is melted, add the cumin seeds and millet. (If you're substituting ground cumin, add it when you add the broth.) When the cumin begins to sizzle, and the millet smells nutty, about 3 to 4 minutes, add the onion and celery. Cook for 5 minutes, stirring frequently, or until the onion is soft and translucent.

Add the vegetable broth, salt, turmeric, coriander, ground ginger and cinnamon. Bring the mixture to a boil. Reduce the heat to low, add the golden raisins and prunes, cover and simmer for 20 to 30 minutes, or until the liquid has been absorbed. Remove the millet from the heat and allow it to sit for 10 minutes, then fluff with a fork. Meanwhile, prepare the dressing.

To make the dressing, in a blender or food processor, combine the olive oil, tahini, lemon juice, sea salt, black pepper and the whole garlic cloves from the roasting pan. Blend until combined. If the dressing is too thick, add water by the tablespoon (15 ml) until you reach your desired consistency.

Serve the millet with a heap of chopped kale, top with roasted roots mixture and drizzle generously with dressing. Garnish with fresh herbs and slivered almonds if you want a crunch.

Roasted Cauliflower Caesar Bowl with Parmesan Quinoa Crisps

QUINOA | VEGETARIAN OPTION | MAKES 4–6 SERVINGS

This Caesar combines salty quinoa-Parmesan crisps with broccoli and cauliflower florets roasted so crispy, they verge on healthy chip territory. If you're a little creeped by anchovies, this is a sneaky way to reap the essential fatty acid rewards without staring at a tiny fish—they're blended right into the creamy dressing, so you can forget they're there.

Caesar Dressing

1 (2-oz [57-g]) can oil-packed anchovy fillets (omit for vegetarian option)

½ cup (56 g) raw cashews, soaked

Juice from 1 lemon

1 tbsp (15 ml) Dijon mustard

2 tsp (10 ml) Worcestershire sauce

1 tsp garlic powder

¾ cup (177 ml) avocado oil or olive oil

1 tbsp (3 g) fresh parsley, plus more to taste

Sea salt

Quinoa Crisps

1 cup (180 g) shredded Parmesan

Zest of 1 lemon

Ground black pepper, to taste

1 cup (161 g) cooked quinoa

Roasted Vegetable Sheet Pan

2 medium broccoli, cut into florets, stems peeled and cut into ½-inch (13-mm) rounds

1 head cauliflower, cut into florets

1 bunch green onions, trimmed above the root and chopped

¼ cup (60 ml) avocado oil

Zest of 2 medium lemons

1 tsp crushed red pepper flakes

½ tsp garlic powder

Sea salt and freshly ground pepper

To Serve

Chopped kale

4 cups (644 g) cooked quinoa

Chopped flat-leaf parsley

Shaved and grated Parmesan

To make the Caesar dressing, blend the anchovies, cashews, lemon juice, mustard, Worcestershire sauce, garlic powder, avocado oil and parsley in a high-speed blender or food processor until the nuts are finely ground and the mixture is creamy. Season with salt, and thin with additional oil and/or water until your desired consistency is reached. Store in an airtight container in the refrigerator.

To make the quinoa crisps, preheat the oven to 425°F (220°C) and line a sheet pan with parchment paper. In a mixing bowl, whisk together the shredded cheese, lemon zest and ground black pepper. Stir in the cooked quinoa. Scoop ½ tablespoon (5 g) of the mixture onto the sheet pan, and press into thin "chips." Arrange the chips in an even layer and bake for 20 minutes. Remove from the oven, flip the chips and cook until crispy, about 10 more minutes. Transfer to a cooling rack to cool.

To make the roasted vegetable sheet pan, increase the oven heat to 450°F (230°C). Line a large rimmed baking sheet with parchment paper. In a large mixing bowl, toss the broccoli, cauliflower florets and chopped green onion with the oil, lemon zest, red pepper flakes, garlic powder and salt and pepper. Spread the mixture in an even layer on a sheet pan. Cut the zested lemons in half and add to the pan, cut side up. Roast for 15 minutes, then remove from the oven, and give the veggies a good stir. Return to the oven, and roast until the vegetables are crispy and caramelized, about 10 to 15 minutes more. Once cool enough to handle, squeeze the roasted lemon juice over the veggies.

To serve, fill a bowl with the chopped kale. Sprinkle with the cooked quinoa, then top with the roasted veggies and a couple of quinoa crisps. Top with the chopped flat-leaf parsley and Parmesan, then drizzle with dressing.

TIPS & TRICKS

Double the batch of quinoa crisps, and save them for a snack or to serve with a cheese board. They pair well with creamy cheeses and fruits or with hummus. For an even crunchier variation, use a roasted kale as an accent instead of the base. Try this recipe with roasted or grilled chicken, salmon or arctic charr for other meal prep variations.

Guacamole Rice Bowl with Buffalo Cauliflower Bites

BROWN RICE, CORNMEAL, TEFF FLOUR | VEGETARIAN | MAKES 4–6 SERVINGS

When it comes to grain bowls, the grains are all too often an afterthought. It's understandable, since the many whole grain options have so many flavor and texture nuances. However, in this bowl, the avocado-based green sauce, which would cost you *way* extra at Chipotle, is mixed right into the rice to create a colorful guacamole-like base for a healthy, vegetarian take on chicken wings!

Buffalo Cauliflower Bites

½ cup (65 g) teff flour

½ cup (85 g) cornmeal/masa harina

1 cup (240 ml) buttermilk

¼ tsp garlic powder

¼ tsp ground turmeric

¼ tsp sea salt

¼ tsp ground black pepper

1 head cauliflower (4–5 cups [918–1147 g] florets)

¾ cup (177 ml) Sriracha

Rice Bowl and Sauce

1 cup (210 g) long grain brown rice

2 cups (480 ml) vegetable broth

1 avocado, peeled and pitted

1 jalapeño, seeded

2 cloves garlic, minced

1½ cups (60 g) cilantro leaves

½ cup (20 g) flat-leaf parsley leaves

Zest and juice of 3 limes

¼ cup (60 ml) avocado oil, plus more for drizzling

Salt and pepper, to taste

To Serve

Shredded cabbage or slaw

Chopped fresh cilantro

Cotija or feta cheese

Greek yogurt or sour cream

To make the cauliflower bites, preheat the oven to 450°F (230°C). Whisk the teff flour, cornmeal, buttermilk, garlic powder, ground turmeric, salt and pepper together until they form a paste. Dip the cauliflower pieces into the batter, using your hands to pat the mixture into place.

Place the coated florets on a parchment paper–lined baking sheet. Repeat until all of the cauliflower florets have been battered. Bake on an upper rack for 15 to 20 minutes until lightly crisped and browned. (Meanwhile, start the rice.) Remove the pan from the heat, and gently toss the florets in a bowl with the Sriracha. Return to the pan, and bake for another 15 to 20 minutes, until extra crispy.

To make the rice, place the rice in a large strainer or colander and rinse it thoroughly under cool water. Warm a saucepan over medium-high heat. Add the rice and toast until the rice is dry and looks slightly toasted on the tips, about 2 to 3 minutes. It will also smell fragrant and nutty. Slowly pour the vegetable broth into the rice. Bring to a boil, then reduce the heat to low, cover and simmer for 45 minutes. Remove the rice from the heat. Let the rice stand another 10 to 15 minutes, covered to prevent the rice from becoming overly sticky.

While the rice sits, prepare the green sauce. In a food processor or blender, combine the avocado, jalapeño, garlic, cilantro, parsley, lime zest, lime juice and oil, and blend until smooth. Set aside.

Uncover the rice, and fluff with a fork. Drizzle with the avocado oil, then stir in the green sauce. Season with salt and pepper. Keep warm until ready to serve.

To serve, add a scoop of green rice to a bowl, and top with shredded cabbage or slaw, cauliflower florets, fresh cilantro, cheese and a dollop of yogurt or sour cream.

Cacao-Rubbed Cabbage with Citrus Salsa

SORGHUM AND/OR WILD RICE │ VEGAN │ MAKES 4–6 SERVINGS

One of my friends, who happens to be one of my favorite vegan chefs, has a very visible tattoo of meat on a grilling fork on his forearm. He's equally known for spending hours, if not *days*, transforming raw meat into fall-off-your-fork roasts, as he is for creating "Buddha burgers" that could convince meat eaters to give legumes a chance. It was precisely his understanding of technique and flavor that made him a skillful vegetable whisperer.

I'm not saying you *have* to eat meat to eat *well*, but if you do eat meat, there are opportunities to shift your thinking when it comes to vegetarian dishes, which can lead to an increase in vegetable intake—a win! Case in point, this grain bowl treats cabbage "steaks" like chicken or fish, coating them with a spice rub that roasts into their layers and puts a completely different twist on a vegan bowl.

Cacao-Rubbed Cabbage

Avocado oil, for greasing

2 tbsp (24 g) coconut sugar or light brown sugar

2 tsp (5 g) raw cacao or cocoa powder

2 tsp (5 g) ground coriander

1 tsp smoked paprika

¾ tsp sea salt

¼–½ tsp cayenne pepper

1 medium red cabbage, cut into thick rings or "steaks"

Citrus Salsa

1 medium shallot, diced

¼ cup (60 ml) red-wine vinegar

¼ tsp sea salt

2 large navel oranges

2 grapefruits, peeled and chopped

2 cups (270 g) pomegranate seeds

1 cup (40 g) chopped mint

¼ cup (10 g) chopped fresh parsley

¼ cup (60 ml) extra virgin olive oil

To Serve

4 cups (682 g) cooked sorghum and/or wild rice

1–2 fennel bulbs, sliced thin

To make the cabbage, position a rack in the lower third of the oven and preheat to 450°F (230°C). Grease a sheet pan with oil and set aside.

In a small bowl, combine the coconut sugar, cacao, coriander, paprika, salt and cayenne. Note: ½ teaspoon of cayenne adds a definite kick, so if you prefer less heat, reduce that quantity. Rub the spice mixture on the cabbage steaks, then arrange on the baking sheet. Roast until the cabbage is crispy, about 20 to 25 minutes. While the cabbage roasts, prepare the salsa.

To make the citrus salsa, combine the shallot, vinegar and salt in a small bowl. Let stand for 5 minutes. Zest the oranges. Cut off and discard the peels and white pith, then coarsely chop the fruit. Add the zest, chopped oranges, chopped grapefruit, pomegranate seeds, mint, parsley and oil to the shallot, and stir to combine.

To serve, top the grains with the layers of roasted cabbage, raw fennel slices and a generous serving of citrus salsa.

> **TIPS & TRICKS**
> *Of course, if you are a meat eater, you can use this spice rub on meats too. Try it on chicken or fish for non-vegetarian options.*

Sweet Beet Bowl with Curry Chicken & Berry Salsa

BUCKWHEAT GROATS AND/OR QUINOA | MAKES 4–6 SERVINGS

As a food stylist, I'm constantly thinking about how a dish will *look*, but when it comes to adding colorful fruits and vegetables, this thinking is not in vain. "Eat the rainbow," is common advice to encourage eating a range of produce and avoid falling into routines. This colorful bowl offers a blend of raw fruit and fresh mint over a supersaturated, roasted beet and buckwheat base. It's visually appealing *and* nutritionally beneficial.

The recipe uses buckwheat groats, but they do have a stronger, earthier flavor than your other grains. If you want to dip your toes and not take a plunge, reduce the buckwheat groats quantity, and mix the groats with a more familiar option like rice or quinoa.

Buckwheat Groats

2 cups (340 g) buckwheat
3½ cups (828 ml) water

Roasted Beets

3 large beets
1 cup Greek yogurt
Zest of 1 orange
1 tsp ground ginger
½ tsp turmeric
¼ tsp garlic powder
Avocado oil

Curry Chicken

1½ lb (330 g) boneless, skinless chicken breasts, cut in halves (horizontally)
Tandoori masala seasoning (or curry powder)
Garlic powder
Onion powder
Salt and pepper
Coconut oil cooking spray

Berry Salsa

1½ cups (227 g) chopped strawberries
1 cup (151 g) chopped blackberries
2 jalapeños, seeded, diced
1 cup (40 g) finely chopped mint
Juice of 1 orange
Salt and pepper

To Serve

Fresh greens, like baby spinach
Fresh mint
Goat cheese or bleu cheese

To make the groats, in a medium saucepan, bring the water and buckwheat to a boil. Remove from the heat. Cover and let stand for 10 minutes, or until most of the liquid is absorbed and the buckwheat is soft and chewy. Drain any excess liquid. Set aside.

To make the roasted beets, preheat the oven to 400°F (204°C). Rinse the unpeeled beets with water, then transfer them to a parchment paper-lined roasting pan. Place in the oven and roast for 35 to 40 minutes, or until the beets have softened. Remove from the oven and cool completely.

Peel the skin away from the roasted beet (wear gloves if you want to avoid beet-stained hands), and transfer the beets to a food processor or blender. Pulse to coarsely chop the beets. Add the Greek yogurt, orange zest, ground ginger, turmeric and garlic powder, and purée. Drizzle the buckwheat groats with avocado oil, then pour the beet mixture over the grains, stirring to fully incorporate. Set aside.

To make the curry chicken, pat the chicken dry with paper towels, then sprinkle with an even coating of tandoori masala, garlic powder and onion powder. Season the chicken with salt and pepper, then spray with coconut oil or drizzle with more avocado oil.

Heat a grill pan or a nonstick skillet over medium-high heat. Sauté the chicken until golden brown and cooked through, about 10 to 12 minutes, flipping periodically. Transfer the chicken to a cutting board to cool, then chop into small chunks and let cool.

To make the berry salsa, combine the strawberries, blackberries, jalapeños, mint, orange juice, salt and pepper in a bowl.

To serve, spoon the beet buckwheat into a bowl, add fresh greens and additional mint, top with a chicken breast and berry salsa. Sprinkle with cheese.

> **TIPS & TRICKS**
> *This same chicken preparation adds a spiced twist to the Quinoa-Curry Chicken Salad (page 137). If you want to maximize your meal prep, increase the chicken quantity, and you're en route to an appetizer/dinner option as well.*

Weeknight Mains

Whole Grains, Not A Whole Lot of Time

Get ready to change up your weeknight eats with meals that can come together in the midst of a busy schedule. If you start your week cooking big batches of grains for grain bowl prepping, these recipes come together even faster. Protein-rich quinoa makes a vegetarian fritter taco (Quinoa "Fish" Fritter Tacos, page 93) that tastes surprisingly like a fried fish taco without anything fake or processed. When toasted and used as a batter, quinoa adds a fried texture to pickle-brined chicken tenders (Pickle-Brined Oven-"Fried" Chicken Tenders with Hot Honey Mustard, page 94), which you'll want to dip generously. A cornmeal batter achieves a similar crispy, fried-like texture for a weeknight cod bake (Spicy Cod & Chorizo Bake, page 109) and the classic Sloppy Joe reinvents itself using millet and lentils for a meaty, barbeque flavor atop a roasted sweet potato (Harissa-Spiced Sloppy Joe Sweet Potatoes, page 104). Dip into all your favorite nacho toppings with a protein-packed quinoa jalapeño chip (Friday Night Nachos, page 106) that calls for a TGIF movie night and margaritas. Cheers, friends!

Quinoa "Fish" Fritter Tacos

BROWN RICE FLOUR, QUINOA | VEGETARIAN | MAKES 15–17 FRITTERS

I'm not one to emulate meats in vegetarian cooking, preferring to let vegetables shine in their own right. However, this fritter just *happens* to taste like a fish taco that could fool your meat-eating friends. There's no fake meats, soy or processed foods, but there is protein, thanks to the quinoa. That's the power of quinoa, vegetables and herbs. They'll transform your next Taco Tuesday into a Meatless Monday. You follow?

Quinoa Fritters

⅔ cup (112 g) quinoa, rinsed, drained

1⅓ cups (315 ml) filtered water or vegetable stock

1 (8.5-oz [240-g]) can artichoke hearts

1 red onion, finely diced

½ cup (20 g) chopped cilantro

¼ cup (10 g) chopped flat-leaf parsley

2 cloves garlic, minced

1 tsp sea salt

Freshly ground black pepper

½ tsp smoked paprika

Juice of 1 lime

½ cup (76 g) brown rice flour (or millet or teff)

1 large egg

1 large egg yolk

Avocado oil, for frying

To Serve

Corn tortillas or gluten-free tortilla of choice

Cabbage slaw

Salsa

Torn cilantro leaves

Sliced avocado or guacamole

Lime wedges

Greek yogurt or sour cream

Spicy mayo

Heat a dry medium saucepan over high heat. Add the quinoa and cook, stirring constantly, until toasted and golden brown, about 5 minutes. Add the water or stock and bring to a boil. Reduce the heat to a simmer, cover and cook until the quinoa is tender and the water is absorbed, 10 to 15 minutes. Remove from the heat and let stand, covered, for 5 minutes.

Drain the artichoke hearts and transfer to a large bowl. Use a fork and knife to shred the artichoke hearts until no large chunks remain (longer shreds are fine).

Add the onion, cilantro, parsley, garlic, salt, pepper, paprika and lime juice to the artichoke, and stir to combine.

Add the flour to the quinoa; toss to coat. Add the egg and egg yolk, then stir the quinoa mixture into the artichoke mixture, until a dough forms (mix gently to prevent the quinoa from breaking apart).

Scoop up some dough with a soup spoon; use a second spoon to scoop dough out of the first spoon, smoothing and forming dough into an oval shape. Repeat until a football-like shape forms (you just made what chefs call a "quenelle"), or more simply, use a small ice cream scoop to create scoops. Place the quenelles (or scoops) on a large plate or baking sheet and repeat with remaining dough.

Pour the oil into a large heavy skillet to a depth of ½-inch (13-mm), about 2 cups (480 ml). Heat the oil over medium-high heat.

Working in batches, place the quenelles in the oil and fry, turning occasionally, until cooked through and all sides are golden, 4 to 5 minutes. Using a slotted spoon, transfer the quinoa fritters to paper towels to drain.

Serve the quenelles in corn tortillas with cabbage slaw, salsa, fresh cilantro, sliced avocado or guacamole, a lime squeeze, Greek yogurt and spicy mayo.

Pickle-Brined Oven-"Fried" Chicken Tenders with Hot Honey Mustard

BROWN RICE FLOUR, QUINOA | MAKES 8 SERVINGS

Lunch on my grandparents' farm began immediately after breakfast was cleared. Grandma Wagner took nourishing and nurturing very seriously, values that extended beyond her own table and into her community. As she did the dishes, she put the lunch plans into action, and if those actions hinted at fried chicken, we knew we were in for a treat!

Grandpa and my uncles would return from the farm fields to Grandma's long table, where we eagerly devoured her legendary fried chicken, staple cucumber salad and corn and tomatoes from her garden. Almost boastfully, my sisters and I pushed away our plates, full and pleased, but my grandpa's next action drew a line in the *field* and showed us that we were clearly city folk. He gnawed on the little bits of chicken we had left on the bone, then used a slice of bread to wipe the grease off our plates and take a hearty bite. He showed us! Grandpa Lawrence lived well into his 90s, eating well and walking his fields with jokes to spare and hugs aplenty. He was a real example of an earnest life.

This oven-"fried" chicken is a wholesome, whole grain way to eat a crusty piece of chicken without the mess of frying. The pickle brine is a little trick I picked up from a local chef (thanks Fiore Moletz!). It's a resourceful way to use the pickling juices leftover after the pickles have been consumed, so in the spirit of my grandpa, you can waste less and enjoy more!

1½ lbs (680 g) boneless, skinless chicken breasts

1½–2 cups (355–473 ml) dill pickle juice (enough to cover the chicken)

¾ cup (128 g) quinoa

1½ cups (355 ml) vegetable broth

½ tsp onion powder

½ tsp garlic powder

½ tsp dried herbs de Provence

¼ tsp sea salt, plus more for seasoning the top

¼ tsp ground black pepper

Spray oil, such as coconut oil for greasing pan

¼ cup (38 g) brown rice flour

¼ cup (32 g) arrowroot starch/flour

2 eggs

Hot Honey Mustard Dipping Sauce

⅓ cup (78 ml) honey

⅓ cup (78 ml) Dijon mustard

3 tbsp (45 ml) Sriracha

(continued)

To marinate the chicken, slice the chicken in half horizontally to create more even shaped pieces (you can also trim them into traditional chicken tender strips if you want a more dippable end result), then transfer to a shallow bowl. Cover the chicken with enough pickle juice to submerge the pieces completely. Marinate in the refrigerator for at least 8 hours (I like to put mine in the fridge the night before for maximum pickle infusion). After marinating, drain and dry the chicken completely on paper towels, and discard the pickle juice. Keep the chicken refrigerated until ready to batter.

Preheat the oven to 400°F (204°C).

To prepare the quinoa, in a fine mesh strainer, rinse the quinoa under water for 1 to 2 minutes. Heat a saucepan over medium-high heat. Add the rinsed quinoa and cook, stirring constantly, to let the water evaporate and toast the quinoa, about 1 minute. Stir in the vegetable broth, onion powder, garlic powder, herbs de Provence, salt and pepper, and bring to a rolling boil. Reduce the heat to low, cover and cook for 15 minutes. Remove the pot from the heat and let stand for 5 more minutes, covered. Fluff with a fork, then transfer the quinoa to a baking sheet in an even layer. Bake at 400°F (204°C) for 15 to 20 minutes to toast. Remove from the oven and let cool slightly.

To batter the chicken, increase the oven temperature to 425°F (220°C). Grease a sheet pan with coconut oil. Set out 2 deep mixing bowls or pie pans and the tray of crispy quinoa. In the first pan, whisk together the brown rice flour and arrowroot starch. In the second, whisk the eggs.

Pat each piece of chicken dry with paper towels. Moisture will prevent the batter from sticking properly. Roll and press the chicken pieces into the flour mixture, coating thoroughly, even in the crevices. This will help the chicken to get extra crispy. Dip the floured piece in the beaten egg, then roll and press into the crispy quinoa. Transfer to a sheet pan and repeat until all of the pieces are battered, leaving space between the pieces. Spray the chicken with coconut oil.

Bake for 20 to 25 minutes, until the quinoa crust is golden brown, and the chicken juices run clear (not pink) when poked with a sharp knife, or the internal temperature of the chicken breasts is 165°F (74°C).

To make the sauce, whisk together the honey, Dijon mustard and Sriracha in a small bowl. Serve the chicken with the dipping sauce, and enjoy!

Amaranth Kimchi Pancakes

AMARANTH, OAT OR BROWN RICE FLOUR | VEGETARIAN | MAKES 10–12 PANCAKES

Forging food adventures solo can lead to some very comical (i.e. *painful*) experiences, e.g. the very first time I had wasabi. Sitting outside, waiting for a class to start, I settled into my first sushi experience. (You know where this is going!) "What's this green purée?" I thought innocently, while obviously scooping a *spoonful* into my mouth. Even *writing* those words makes my sinuses start to drain. As I panic slurped my smoothie, I was immensely grateful I had decided to eat *before* class and not during. If only someone had intervened and said, "Easy there tiger, that stuff will knock your nose off!"

Since that sinus cleanse, I've relied more heavily on friends and waiters to guide me into new cuisines. These savory pancakes were inspired by eggy Korean pancakes and Japanese okonomiyaki, but the base is the Aztec's ancient grain: cooked amaranth. Amaranth's creamy texture yields a very spongy, savory pancake, which works well in contrast to the crunch of the kimchi and chopped nuts.

Adding these amaranth pancakes to your weeknight dinner rotation also helps to boost your vitamin B6 intake. B vitamins help to produce serotonin, so after a good meal, you're in for a good sleep cycle. They also help to stabilize your mood, so you just might play it cool if you accidentally ingest a scoop of wasabi. No promises on that front though.

Amaranth Pancakes
3 cups (709 ml) vegetable broth
1 cup (170 g) amaranth
2 eggs
2 tbsp (19 g) oat flour or brown rice flour
½ cup (170 g) kimchi, chopped (see Tips & Tricks on page 98)
Sesame oil, for greasing

Sauce
½ cup (120 ml) maple syrup
½ cup (120 ml) ketchup
2 tbsp (29 g) fresh grated ginger
1 tbsp (15 ml) sesame oil
2 cloves garlic, minced
¼ tsp ground black pepper
¼ tsp ground allspice
⅛ tsp ground cloves

Wasabi Avocado Crema
1 tsp wasabi powder, or more, to taste
1 tbsp (15 ml) lime juice
1 ripe avocado
½ cup (123 g) plain Greek yogurt
½ cup (20 g) chopped cilantro
½ tsp sea salt

To Serve
Extra kimchi
Scallions, chopped
Chopped roasted cashews
Fresh cilantro
Fresh limes

(continued)

Amaranth Kimchi Pancakes (continued)

To make the pancakes, bring the broth to a boil in a pot and add the amaranth. Cover, reduce the heat and simmer until the water is absorbed, about 20 minutes. Set aside to cool, then drain off any liquid that remains on the surface, then stir.

In the bowl of a stand mixer, beat the eggs until slightly frothy. Add the amaranth and oat flour, and beat until combined. Fold in the chopped kimchi.

Place a parchment paper–lined sheet pan in the oven, and heat to the warm setting. Heat a griddle over medium heat. Fold a sheet of paper towel in half and moisten it with sesame oil; carefully rub the skillet with the oiled paper towel. Scoop ¼ cup (60 ml) of the amaranth batter onto the heated griddle, using the back of a spoon or small spatula to smooth the thick batter into a circle.

Cook until the surface of the pancakes have several bubbles and the edges are firm, about 2 minutes. Use a thin spatula to flip, and cook until browned on the underside, about 1 to 2 minutes. Transfer to the warm oven, and repeat with the remaining batter, greasing the skillet as necessary.

To make the sauce, add the maple syrup, ketchup, ginger, sesame oil, garlic, black pepper, allspice and cloves to a saucepan over medium heat, and cook until syrupy and reduced, 4 to 6 minutes. Strain out the cloves and set the sauce aside.

To make the crema, dissolve the wasabi powder in the lime juice in a medium bowl. Add the avocado and mash well. Add the Greek yogurt, cilantro and salt and stir until blended. For a more consistent texture, you can use a food processor. Keep chilled until ready to use.

To serve, drizzle the sauce over the pancake. Top with extra kimchi and a dollop of wasabi crema. Garnish with the scallions, chopped nuts and fresh cilantro. Add a squeeze of lime and enjoy.

TIPS & TRICKS

Kimchi is traditionally made with fish sauce, so if you want to keep this as a vegetarian option, be sure to buy a jar that is designated vegan or vegetarian. For the sauce, use a low-sugar ketchup. A side of extra roasted broccoli with oil and red pepper flakes makes a healthy pairing for these flavors. Serve it on the side or as a pancake topper.

Salmon-Sardine Cakes with Mango-Cabbage Slaw

OAT FLOUR OR BROWN RICE FLOUR, QUINOA | MAKES 8–10 SERVINGS

In preparation for a trip-of-a-lifetime to Kenya, I received all of the recommended vaccines, had the weird dreams associated with antimalarials, made sure my passport was up to date and then settled into a Swahili alphabet book called *Jambo Means Hello.* The two words that stuck with me were *jambo* and *embe* (mango). If nothing else, I'd be able to feed my mango obsession right from the source. "Hello, mango?" and "Hello, mango!" seemed like they could get me pretty far (in conjunction with all my friendly translators).

Mango makes this salad bright, colorful and refreshing and adds a tart contrast to the Salmon-Sardine Cake. Sardines have been gaining popularity for their health benefits (omega 3s, vitamin B12 and vitamin D), but there's still a lot of hesitation around canned fish. This salmon cake is a way to eat more sardines on the sly. Paired with high-protein quinoa and oat flour instead of panko, these nutrient-rich cakes pack layers of flavor and textures that will leave you saying, "Hello, sardines!"

Cabbage Slaw

2 cups (681 g) shredded red cabbage

4 cups (1.4 kg) shredded carrots (about 2 large carrots)

2 champagne mangos, peeled and sliced

1 cup (40 g) chopped basil

Salmon Cakes

2 tbsp (30 g) coconut oil or unsalted butter, plus more for greasing

2 cups (302 g) chopped yellow onion

3 cloves garlic

1 jalapeño, seeded and diced

Zest of 1 lime

1 tsp fresh grated ginger

1 cup (170 g) cooked quinoa

16 oz (454 g) raw salmon, skin removed

2 (3.75-oz [168-g dry weight]) cans sardines in spring water

2 eggs

1 cup (152 g) oat flour or brown rice flour

½ cup (20 g) chopped cilantro

½ cup (20 g) chopped parsley

Apple Cider Vinaigrette

⅓ cup (78 ml) olive oil

¼ cup (60 ml) apple cider vinegar

Juice and zest of 2 limes

1 tbsp (15 ml) mustard

1 tbsp (15 ml) honey

1 tbsp (15 g) fresh grated turmeric

1 tbsp (15 g) fresh grated ginger

½ tsp black pepper

½ tsp salt

1 tbsp (10 g) flaxseeds

To Serve

Avocado crema or guacamole

Fresh cilantro

Crushed roasted cashews, peanuts or pistachios

To make the slaw, combine the shredded red cabbage, carrots, mango slices and basil in a large salad bowl. Set aside.

To make the salmon cakes, preheat the oven to 400°F (204°C). Line a sheet pan with parchment paper and grease lightly with melted coconut oil. Set aside.

Heat the coconut oil in a large saucepan over medium heat until melted. Add the onions and garlic, and cook, stirring, until onions are soft and starting to turn translucent, 1 to 2 minutes. Add the jalapeño and continue to cook, stirring every few minutes to prevent sticking, until the onions are blonde-colored and starting to brown, 10 to 15 minutes. If the onions start to get too dark or stick to the pan, add a splash of water. Add the lime zest, grated ginger and cooked quinoa, and stir constantly, until the quinoa starts to crisp slightly, about 3 to 5 minutes. Turn off the heat and set aside.

In a food processor, pulse the salmon and sardines until blended but some larger salmon chunks remain. Transfer the fish to a large mixing bowl, then pulse the eggs in the food processor just until texture is consistent. Pour the liquid egg over the fish mixture, followed by the lime juice and quinoa mixture. Stir to combine.

Add the oat flour and stir to combine, until the mixture starts to hold together. Fold in the chopped herbs. Shape the mixture into 9 patties, spaced evenly on the sheet pan. Bake for 10 minutes, remove from oven, flip, then bake for another 10 minutes, until golden brown. While the salmon cakes bake, make the salad dressing.

To make the vinaigrette, combine the oil, vinegar, lime juice, lime zest, mustard, honey, turmeric, ginger, black pepper and salt in a blender or food processor until smooth. Stir in the flaxseeds. Keep chilled until ready to use.

To serve, add a heap of slaw to a bowl or plate. Top with a salmon cake and a dollop of avocado crema or guacamole, fresh cilantro and chopped nuts. Add the dressing to taste.

> ### TIPS & TRICKS
> *Top the salmon cakes with an egg, and you have a brunch dish. Mix leftover slaw with quinoa or rice, and you have a grain bowl lunch in the making.*

Sweet Summer Caprese with Blue Corn Polenta

CORNMEAL | VEGETARIAN | MAKES 4–6 SERVINGS

Roasting brings out the innate sweetness of seasonal tomatoes and peaches. Combined with creamy polenta, this recipe elevates the classic caprese salad into a main dish fit for easy summer entertaining.

Polenta is just a more official way of saying cornmeal mush, so don't get hung up on terminology when grocery shopping. It can be made with any kind of cornmeal: ground coarse, medium or fine, but to contrast the bright reds and oranges of the roasted fruits, I recommend an unexpected twist: blue cornmeal polenta. Your guests will eat with their eyes for a moment, but ultimately, they'll be scraping down their bowls.

Caprese

Avocado oil, for greasing

3 lbs (1.4 kg) assorted cherry, plum and/ or grape tomatoes, halved

4 medium peaches (1 lb [454 g]), sliced

4 shallots, quartered

1 head of garlic, peeled and separated

Smoked sea salt or regular sea salt

1 bunch thyme (about 20 sprigs)

1 (15-oz [425-g]) can white beans or cannellini or Great Northern

Blue Corn Polenta

4 cups (946 ml) water or vegetable stock

1 tsp salt

1 cup (170 g) blue cornmeal

1–2 tbsp (15–30 g) butter or olive oil

½ cup (20 g) chopped fresh basil

½ cup (90 g) grated Parmesan

Crushed black pepper, to taste

Basil Vinaigrette

1 cup (40 g) loosely packed, chopped fresh basil leaves

1½ cups (355 ml) extra virgin olive oil

1 tbsp (15 ml) balsamic vinegar

2 tsp (10 ml) honey

2 tsp (10 ml) Dijon mustard

½ tsp ground pepper

¼ tsp salt

To Serve

8 oz (227 g) fresh mozzarella cheese, at room temperature

Fresh basil

To make the caprese, position a rack in the middle of the oven and preheat the oven to 375°F (190°C). Drizzle a sheet pan with oil, and arrange the tomatoes cut side up. Add the peach slices, shallot quarters and garlic cloves (you can leave them whole or mince them, depending on your garlic eating preferences). Sprinkle the sheet pan with smoked sea salt, and top with the thyme sprigs.

Roast for 40 minutes, tossing once. Meanwhile, prepare the cornmeal polenta.

To make the polenta, add the water or stock to a 2- to 3-quart (1.9- to 2.8-L) pot with lid, and bring to a boil over medium-high heat. Add the salt. Pour the cornmeal in a steady stream into the boiling water, whisking gently as you pour. Continue whisking until the cornmeal has thickened, about 3 minutes. Cover the pot and continue cooking for 40 minutes, stirring vigorously every 10 minutes, scraping the sides and bottoms of the pan. Once the polenta has cooked fully, you can add a drizzle of olive oil or butter for extra flavor, and stir in the chopped basil and Parmesan. Season with black pepper to taste.

After 40 minutes, remove the tomato mixture from the oven. Increase the oven temperature to 400°F (204°C). Remove the shallots, and set aside. Add the white beans evenly over the tray, and roast until the tomatoes are caramelized, about 20 minutes. Turn off the oven, and keep the oven door propped open slightly to let the tomato mixture cool slightly. Meanwhile, prepare the vinaigrette.

To make the vinaigrette, combine the roasted shallot, basil, oil, balsamic vinegar, honey, mustard, pepper and salt in a blender, and purée until smooth. You can make the vinaigrette ahead, then refrigerate. The vinaigrette will discolor slightly after refrigeration, but will remain flavorful.

To serve, spoon the polenta into a bowl, top with the tomatoes and peaches, add the fresh mozzarella, fresh basil and a generous drizzle of vinaigrette.

> ### TIPS & TRICKS
> *Leftover polenta will solidify and take the shape of its container after refrigeration. To restore the creamy texture, simply warm it with a little broth or water, and stir vigorously.*

Harissa-Spiced Sloppy Joe Sweet Potatoes

MILLET | VEGAN | MAKES 4–6 SERVINGS

The night I introduced my boyfriend to my parents, we didn't eat prime rib, slow-cooked chuck roast or grilled steaks. We gathered at the dining room table, and we ate sloppy Joes. The casual choice seemed to say, "It's as if we've always known you, Kyle. Welcome home!"

They're not fancy. They're not high brow, but if church halls, VFWs and good ol' chuck wagons teach us anything, it's that sloppy Joes can *really* bring people together. Odds are, you're not entertaining a congregation, so you can take some risks (i.e. sandwich sacrilege), ditch the meat, skip the bun and serve this classic American mess on a maple and spice-roasted sweet potato. The lentils and millet in this vegan version not only mimic the texture of ground beef, but they're high in protein, affordable and easy to keep on hand for weeknight meal prep.

Spice-Roasted Sweet Potatoes

2 large sweet potatoes, halved lengthwise

3 tbsp (45 ml) melted coconut oil, divided

1 tsp chili powder

1 tsp smoked paprika

1 tsp harissa spice mix

1 tsp sumac, optional

Sea salt and cracked black pepper

2 tbsp (30 ml) maple syrup

2 limes, halved

Sloppy Joes

2 tbsp (30 ml) coconut oil

1 cup (152 g) chopped white onion

3 cloves garlic, minced

1 tsp smoked paprika

1/2 tsp cumin

1 red bell pepper, chopped

1/2 cup (100 g) green lentils

1/2 cup (85 g) millet

2 1/2 cups (592 ml) vegetable broth

6 oz (170 g) tomato paste

1/2 cup (118 ml) ketchup

1/4 cup (60 ml) apple cider vinegar

3 tbsp (45 ml) harissa sauce

2 tbsp (30 ml) Worcestershire sauce

1 tbsp (15 ml) liquid amino acids or gluten-free soy sauce, optional

1 tsp Dijon mustard

Sea salt and black pepper, to taste

To Serve

Chopped green onion

Fresh cilantro

To make the sweet potatoes, preheat the oven to 425°F (220°C). Line a sheet pan with parchment paper. Brush the surfaces of the sweet potatoes, including the skins, with 1 tablespoon (15 ml) of melted coconut oil, then arrange cut-side up on the pan.

In a small bowl or ramekin, combine 2 tablespoons (30 ml) of melted coconut oil and the spices until they form a paste. Distribute the paste amongst the 4 potato halves, and season with salt and pepper.

Bake for 40 minutes (you can prepare the filling while the sweet potatoes bake). Remove from the oven, and drizzle each sweet potato half with maple syrup. Bake for another 5 to 10 minutes, until the surfaces are lightly caramelized and the sweet potatoes are tender. Remove from the oven and squeeze fresh lime juice over the surfaces.

To make the sloppy Joes, melt the coconut oil in a large saucepan over medium-high heat. Add the onion and garlic, and sauté until softened, about 5 to 7 minutes, stirring frequently with a wooden spoon or heat-proof spatula.

Add the smoked paprika and cumin, and stir until the spices are evenly distributed and toasted. Add in the red pepper, lentils and millet, stirring to evenly coat the grains. Continue to cook and stir until the millet is toasted, about 5 minutes. You can add a splash of water or broth if anything starts to brown too quickly.

Add the broth, increase the heat to high and bring the liquid to a boil. Reduce the heat, cover and simmer until the legumes and millet have absorbed the liquid, about 15 minutes. Avoid the temptation to uncover the pot and peek. Remove from the heat and let stand, uncovered, for 10 minutes, then fluff with a fork.

Return the pot to low heat, and add the tomato paste, ketchup, apple cider vinegar, harissa sauce, Worcestershire sauce, liquid aminos and Dijon mustard. Stir and bring to a simmer, until slightly thickened, about 5 to 10 minutes. Season with salt and pepper to taste. Keep warm until ready to serve.

To serve, top each sweet potato half with a hearty scoop of sloppy Joe mix. Garnish with chopped green onion and fresh cilantro, and enjoy!

> ### Tips & Tricks
> *Harissa is a traditional North African condiment. It's a garlicky chili sauce, much like a hot sauce, that has been gaining popularity. This recipe uses harissa as both a spice and a sauce. If you can't find the sauce, try adding more ketchup for a mild flavor, or hot sauce or Sriracha for a kick.*

Friday Night Nachos

QUINOA | VEGETARIAN | MAKES 25 QUINOA CRISPS OR 4 NACHO SERVINGS

As much as I aim to eat at the table, to avoid "screen time" and engage in conversation, there is a definite time and place for the opposite, mainly Friday nights, on the couch, with a hearty tray of nachos and a good Netflix lineup.

A far cry from concession stands' plastic trays of bright orange cheese and tortilla chips, these nachos start with a batch of savory quinoa. Mixed with cheese and heat, think of these as a cross between a tortilla chip and a thin latke, but mostly think of them as protein-packed carriers for avocados and melted cheese. You'll have to carry your own margarita though.

Quinoa Crisps

1 cup (170 g) quinoa

2 cups (480 ml) vegetable broth

2 cups (242 g) shredded Mexican cheese blend

Zest of 2 limes

1 tsp cayenne pepper

Freshly ground black pepper, to taste

1 jalapeño, seeded and finely diced or grated

Toppings

Salsa, to taste

1 (15-oz [425-g]) can black beans, rinsed

1–2 avocados

1 red bell pepper, chopped

Mexican cheese blend

To Serve

Greek yogurt or sour cream

Fresh cilantro

To make the quinoa crisps, rinse the quinoa in a fine mesh strainer under water for 1 to 2 minutes. Heat a saucepan over medium-high heat. Add the rinsed quinoa and cook, stirring constantly, to let the water evaporate and toast the quinoa, about 1 minute. Stir in the vegetable broth, and bring to a rolling boil. Reduce the heat to low, cover and cook for 15 minutes. Remove the pot from the heat and let stand for 5 more minutes, covered. Uncover, fluff with a fork, then transfer to a parchment paper–lined sheet pan in an even layer to cool.

Preheat the oven to 425°F (220°C).

In a mixing bowl, whisk together the shredded cheese blend, lime zest, cayenne pepper and ground black pepper. Stir in the cooled quinoa and diced jalapeño, and stir to combine. Replace the parchment paper on the sheet pan. Scoop ½ tablespoon (15 g) of the mixture onto the sheet pan, and press into thin "chips." Arrange the chips in an even layer and bake for 20 minutes. Remove from the oven, flip the chips and cook until crispy, about 10 more minutes. Remove from the oven.

To make the nachos, top the quinoa crisps with salsa, your favorite nacho toppings and cheese, and return to the oven until the cheese is melted. Serve with Greek yogurt or sour cream and fresh cilantro.

Spicy Cod & Chorizo Bake

CORNMEAL, MILLET | MAKES 4 SERVINGS

Entering or exiting my Pittsburgh neighborhood of Polish Hill, one can't help but catch glimpses of the exquisite Polish cathedral, and during lent, one can't help but catch glimpses of fried cod. As much as my boyfriend, my "Rustbelt Farmer," wants to dive into those fish fries, I always resist with my host of kill-joy responses. "Where is the fish from? It's probably frozen. They probably use terrible oils." If I'm going to deny a man a fish fry, I at least have to offer him some cod.

Much like the grain bowl formula, this recipe relies on sheet pans to do the heavy lifting for your dinner. The cod, chorizo and roasted cherry tomatoes pack so much flavor, a simple millet prepared with vegetable broth is not a cop out. It's just the right balance for the spice.

Millet

1 cup (170 g) raw millet

2 cups (480 ml) vegetable broth

1 tbsp (15 g) unsalted butter

Spicy Crispy Cod & Chorizo

4 tbsp (60 ml) avocado oil or high heat oil, divided, plus more for greasing

2 (15-oz [425-g]) cans cannellini beans, rinsed

1½ cups (242 g) cherry tomatoes, halved

1 lb (454 g) chorizo, casing removed and meat chopped into small pieces

4–5 cloves garlic, minced

½ tsp crushed red pepper

1 tsp salt

½ tsp pepper

¼ cup (33 g) arrowroot flour/starch or potato starch

½ tsp onion powder

½ tsp garlic powder

¼ tsp chipotle smoked red jalapeño powder (or chili powder)

¼ tsp ground cumin

2 eggs

¾ cup (128 g) cornmeal

4 (5–6 oz [142–170 g]) boneless, skinless cod fillets

Spray coconut oil or cooking oil

2 limes, cut in half

1 cup (40 g) coarsely chopped cilantro, plus more to serve

To make the millet, toast the raw millet in a large, dry saucepan over medium heat for 4 to 5 minutes, until the grains become fragrant but not burnt. Add the broth, and give the millet a good stir. Increase the heat to high, and bring the mixture to a boil. Once boiling, reduce the heat to low, add the butter and cover the pot. Simmer until the grains absorb most of the broth, about 15 minutes (they'll continue to absorb the liquid as they sit). Remove from the heat and let stand, covered, for 10 minutes. After the millet sits, fluff it with a fork and serve immediately.

To make the cod, position the oven racks on the lower and middle positions. Preheat the oven to 450°F (230°C). Grease two large, rimmed baking sheets with oil. Spread the cannellini beans, cherry tomatoes, chorizo and garlic in an even layer on the first pan. Drizzle with 2 tablespoons (30 ml) of oil, and season with the crushed red pepper, salt and pepper.

Set out 3 deep mixing bowls or pie pans. In the first pan, whisk together the arrowroot, onion powder, garlic powder, chipotle powder (use just a pinch if you want to tone down the spice) and cumin. In the second, whisk the eggs. Add the cornmeal to the third.

Pat each piece of cod dry with paper towels (moisture will prevent the batter from sticking and crisping properly). Season each piece generously with salt. Coat the first fillet thoroughly in the arrowroot mixture, even in crevices, then roll into the egg mixture, and then press into the cornmeal. Transfer to the second sheet pan. Repeat with the remaining pieces of cod, leaving spaces between the cod on the pan. Spray the cod with the coconut oil. Add the limes to the sheet pan cut sides up.

Transfer both sheet pans to the oven, and bake until the cornmeal crust is golden and the fish flakes easily with a fork, 15 to 20 minutes, flipping the fillets halfway through. Remove from oven. Sprinkle with the coarsely chopped cilantro and drizzle with the remaining 2 tablespoons (30 ml) of oil and a squeeze of the roasted limes.

To serve, scoop the warm millet into a bowl. Top with a piece of cod and a mixture of roasted tomatoes and chorizo. Garnish with the cilantro.

Sunday Suppers

Slow Down & Enjoy the Process

Almost a decade ago, I splurged on a copy of the magazine *America's Test Kitchen*. I'm a sucker for beautiful food spreads, as well as the tangibility of magazines, but at the time, the $9.99 price tag was a hefty portion of my food budget. To justify the cost, I vowed to work my way through the pages of the intricate recipes.

Those pages consumed my weekends. I'd wake up early and walk (I didn't have a car at the time and this was pre-Uber!) to Pittsburgh's Strip District to hit the many produce stalls, the public market and the infamous cheese haven, Pennsylvania Macaroni Company. Then, weighed down with food, I'd schlep everything uphill to my apartment, to spend hours bringing those magazine pages to life. They were slow, all-day affairs that resulted in restaurant-worthy dishes. Those pages were my dog-eared, grease-splattered education and planted the seeds for a career in food.

These entrées are the slower sort, so buy that good bottle of wine. They're cause to roll up your sleeves, pick a good soundtrack, exercise a little patience and, hopefully, to set the table for friends and/or family. Mushroom bourguignon (Mushroom Bourguignon with Lemon-Herb Millet, page 123) may not be the classic bourguignon, but ladled over a bed of lemony millet, it will become a new tradition. A side of salmon with beet-roasted parsnips and crunchy sorghum "faux roe" (Beet-Roasted Salmon & Parsnips with Sumac Yogurt & Sorghum Faux Roe, page 117) makes quite the candle-lit centerpiece. Coffee-braised short ribs are so tender they'll melt into the vibrant, minty buckwheat mash (Coffee-Braised Short Ribs with Mint-Pea Buckwheat Mash, page 114). The sorghum and green apple salsa, atop buttery seared scallops (Seared Scallops with Edamame Purée & Tart Sorghum Salsa, page 113), is cause for a date night at home. Let's get cooking, shall we?

Seared Scallops with Edamame Purée & Tart Sorghum Salsa

SORGHUM | MAKES 4 SERVINGS

I come from a long line of landlocked people, which instilled in me a natural comfort in meadows, a healthy respect for the ocean (i.e., fear) and, for a very long time, a seafood "virginity" (because frozen fish sticks smothered in mayo and ketchup are not a proper foray). I approached seafood, as any nerd would—through careful observation, interviews with friends as they tried to eat their mussels in peace and visits to seafood regions. Eventually, I expanded my horizons. Discovering I *liked* scallops was a big deal, but *making* scallops for myself was a *huge* deal!

Whether you're a *landlocker* like myself or grew up surfing monsoons, grab some prosecco or champagne because you're about to put a restaurant-level, plated dish on your table. There are multiple components, but they aren't just for looks. The hearty texture of whole grain sorghum adds a crunch to the make-you-pucker green apple salsa, but it's also an anti-inflammatory, cholesterol-lowering ingredient.

Sorghum Salsa

1 shallot, diced

1 jalapeño pepper, seeded and diced

1 granny smith apple, diced

1 cup (170 g) cooked sorghum

½ cup (20 g) coarsely chopped cilantro

3 tbsp (45 ml) fresh lime juice (about 3 limes)

¼ tsp salt

Edamame Purée

1 tbsp (15 ml) avocado oil

1 small red onion, chopped

3 cloves garlic, chopped

3 cups (603 g) shelled frozen edamame, thawed

¼ cup (60 ml) vegetable stock

Juice and zest of 1 large lemon

2 tbsp (30 g) cold unsalted butter

½ cup (20 g) fresh whole cilantro leaves

Sea salt and freshly ground black pepper

Sea Scallops

1½ lb (680 g) wild caught large "dry" sea scallops (dry scallops are preservative-free)

1 tbsp (15 ml) avocado oil or high-heat oil

Sea salt and freshly ground black pepper

2 tbsp (30 g) unsalted butter, cut into small pieces

4 sprigs thyme

2 tsp (10 ml) fresh lemon juice

To make the sorghum salsa, stir the shallot, jalapeño, apple, cooked sorghum, cilantro, lime juice and salt together in a bowl and set aside.

Meanwhile, place the scallops on a rimmed baking sheet lined with paper towels, blot dry and let sit at room temperature while you make the edamame purée.

To make the edamame purée, heat the avocado oil in a saucepan over medium heat. Add the onion and garlic, and cook until translucent, about 5 to 7 minutes. Add the edamame, vegetable stock, lemon juice and lemon zest, and cook until the edamame is tender, 2 to 3 minutes, stirring frequently. Remove from the heat. Stir in the butter and cilantro.

Using an immersion blender or a food processor, purée the edamame mixture until creamy. Season with salt and pepper to taste, and pulse/blend briefly to combine. Return to the saucepan and cover with a lid to keep warm while you sear the scallops.

To make the scallops, heat the avocado oil in a large skillet over medium-high heat. Season the scallops with salt and pepper, and cook until deep golden brown, about 3 minutes. Flip the scallops, and add butter and thyme to the pan. Spoon the butter over the scallops, and cook until the scallops are cooked through and the butter is brown and smells nutty, about 3 minutes longer. Add the lemon juice.

To serve, spread the edamame purée on a plate. Sprinkle with the sorghum salsa, arrange the scallops and top with additional salsa. Garnish with thyme.

> **TIPS & TRICKS**
> *You'll definitely want a glass of prosecco or a sparkling rosé to complement this dish (and maybe even a glass while cooking).*

Coffee-Braised Short Ribs with Mint-Pea Buckwheat Mash

BUCKWHEAT GROATS | MAKES 4 SERVINGS

This dish is a time commitment, but this is communion with the kitchen at its best. The end result is tender, flaky, almost caramelized beef, parsnips so juicy they burst like a soup dumpling and a mash that contrasts the sweetness of peas with bitter greens and the robust, nuttiness of buckwheat groats.

Short Ribs

2 oz (57 g) coffee beans, ground

1 tsp sea salt

1 tsp black pepper

3 lbs (1.4 kg) grass-fed short ribs, bone-in, about 8 portions

1 tbsp (15 ml) avocado oil or any high-heat oil

2 cups (360 g) medium chopped parsnips

2 celery ribs, chopped (include the greens)

2 medium yellow onions, chopped

2 qt (1.9 L) chicken or vegetable stock

1 cup (240 ml) red wine

6 bay leaves

2 sprigs rosemary

16 peppercorns

Mint-Pea Mash

2 tbsp (30 ml) avocado oil or high-heat oil

2 shallots, finely diced

1 head of garlic, peeled and finely chopped

2 cups (340 g) raw buckwheat groats

4 cups (960 ml) vegetable stock

4 cups (605 g) green peas, divided

4 cups (161 g) chopped dandelion greens

½ cup (20 g) chopped mint leaves

2 tbsp (19 g) lemon zest

Sea salt and pepper, to taste

Pea tendrils or fresh mint, for garnish

To make the short ribs, place the rack on the bottom third of the oven, and preheat the oven to 350°F (177°C). In a shallow mixing bowl, whisk together the ground coffee, sea salt and black pepper. Dip and coat each chunk of meat in the coffee mixture, making sure the rub sticks to all sides. Set aside on a sheet pan.

Heat the oil in a Dutch oven over medium-high heat. Sear the meat on all sides, then return to the sheet pan, and set aside. Keep the Dutch oven over medium-high heat. Add the parsnips, celery and onions, and cook until tender, stirring frequently, about 5 minutes.

Add the stock, wine, bay leaves, rosemary sprigs and peppercorns. Stir to combine and bring to a boil. Once boiling, remove from the heat, and top with the short ribs. Cover and cook in the lower third of the oven for 1½ hours, until the meat is tender but not falling apart. Uncover and braise for 45 minutes, turning the ribs once or twice, until the sauce is reduced by about half and the meat is tender.

Remove from the oven and transfer the meat to a clean shallow baking dish, discarding the bones as they fall off. Strain the sauce into a heatproof measuring cup and skim off as much fat as possible. Pour the sauce over the meat. Place the baking dish under the broiler and baste with glaze until thick and sticky.

To make the mash, heat the oil in a large saucepan or stockpot over medium heat, add the shallots and garlic. Cook until soft and the shallots are translucent, 3 to 4 minutes. Add the buckwheat and cook, stirring, for 2 to 3 minutes, to toast the groats. Increase the heat to medium-high, add the stock and cook, stirring occasionally, for 20 minutes or until absorbed. Meanwhile, combine 2 cups (302 g) of the peas, the dandelion greens, mint and lemon zest in a food processor, and process until mashed—some chunks are okay. Transfer the mash to the pot with the buckwheat, add the remaining peas and stir to combine. Season with salt and pepper to taste.

To serve, top a generous heap of mint-pea buckwheat mash with short ribs. Garnish with the pea tendrils or fresh mint.

Beet-Roasted Salmon & Parsnips with Sumac Yogurt & Sorghum Faux Roe

SORGHUM | MAKES 4–6 SERVINGS

The alternative title for this dish could be "Pretty in Pink," but the beet-infused color isn't just for looks. Beets have long been revered in ayurveda, the 5,000-year-old Indian practice of natural healing, for their ability to cleanse the liver, improve circulation and calm the mind and spirit. If that's too hippy-dippy for you, mainstream nutrition also touts these beet benefits: they're high in antioxidants, relieve inflammation and support digestive health.

All those healthy beet benefits are blended with a horseradish bite, fresh dill and ginger to make an impressive side of salmon. Blending high-fiber sorghum with black olive tapenade not only contrasts the sweetness of the beets, but it creates little pearls that I've dubbed "faux roe" for their caviar-like appearance.

Roasted Salmon

1 large red beet, peeled and cut in chunks

1-inch (2.5-cm) chunk fresh ginger, peeled

1 cup (40 g) dill fronds, chopped, plus more for serving

2 tbsp (30 g) prepared beet horseradish

Grated zest of 1 lemon, plus lemon half for serving

¼ cup (60 ml) avocado oil, divided

1 side wild salmon (1¾–2 lbs [793–907 g]; about 1-inch [2.5-cm] thick at thickest part), skin removed

Sea salt and freshly ground pepper

2 lbs (908 g) parsnips, cut into ¼-inch (6-mm) slices

2 lemons, halved

Sumac Yogurt

2 tbsp (30 ml) olive oil

6 cloves garlic

1 cup (245 g) Greek yogurt

1 tsp ground sumac, optional

Sorghum Faux Roe

½ cup (85 g) cooked sorghum

1 tbsp (11 g) olive tapenade

To Serve

Kale

Fresh dill

To make the salmon, combine the beet chunks, ginger, dill, horseradish, lemon zest and 2 tablespoons (30 ml) of oil in a food processor, and pulse until a paste forms.

Line two rimmed baking sheets with parchment paper. Set one pan aside, and transfer the salmon to the other pan. Season the salmon generously with salt and pepper. Spread the beet mixture on top; it will be a thick layer. Let stand for 30 minutes.

Meanwhile, preheat the oven to 425°F (220°C). In a large mixing bowl, toss the parsnip slices with the remaining 2 tablespoons (30 ml) of oil, and season generously with salt and pepper. Spread the parsnip slices in an even layer on the parchment-lined pan. Add the lemon halves to the pan, cut side up. Bake until the parsnips are tender and starting to crisp, about 50 to 60 minutes; remove from the oven.

Remove the lemons and set aside. Scoop the beet mixture from the top of the salmon, and transfer to the parsnip pan. Toss the parsnips with the beet mixture to coat. Spread the parsnips in an even layer, then the salmon. Drizzle the salmon with additional oil, and bake until the salmon is medium-rare, 10 to 12 minutes. Squeeze the roasted lemon over the surface and set aside while you prepare the yogurt.

To make the sumac yogurt, heat the oil in a saucepan over medium-high heat. Fry the garlic only until they turn a medium brown and then remove from the heat. Watch carefully to avoid burning them. Strain to remove any extra oil. In a small mixing bowl, combine the sautéed garlic, yogurt and sumac.

To make the faux roe, mix the sorghum and olive tapenade in a small bowl until combined. To serve, line a serving platter with fresh kale. Add the salmon and parsnips. Top the salmon with the sumac yogurt and sorghum faux roe. Garnish with the fresh dill.

> **TIPS & TRICKS**
> *Sumac is a traditional Middle Eastern spice made from the red fruits of the namesake trees. They line my neighborhood, and I've long wanted to try creating my own powder, but in the meantime, I've found the packaged version at Whole Foods, online or at ethnic grocers. The flavor is tangy and lemony.*

Eggplant Rollatini with Sorghum Pesto Pearls

SORGHUM | MAKES 4–6 SERVINGS

The absolute fullest I have ever been was after an Easter dinner prepared by my Italian friend's mother. As college students, the home-cooked meal was especially alluring, and the portobello mushrooms and saucy eggplant called my name through thick Italian accents. "Quel-ci, you want to eat-a us! Just-a one-a more bite-a!"

After heeding the mushrooms' call (and a lasagna's call and the bread's call and the cheese's call, etc.), I was so full I just wanted to *die*. I was too full for a reason. In my dramatic delirium, a quick, painless death seemed to be the only viable option to counter such satiation. Thankfully, a nap took me instead, and I powered through the pain unconsciously. Thus, in some pocket of my brain, Italian = pain.

These Eggplant Rollatini are like the Cliff's Notes version of that blissfully painful Easter dinner. They pack some of the key Italian ingredients—eggplant, ricotta, pesto and sun-dried tomatoes—without pushing a near-death level of fullness. The sorghum provides a crunchy contrast to all the creamy fillers. Just remember to leave yourself enough time, since sorghum takes about 60 minutes to prepare, but that texture is worth the wait. Those 60 minutes are also an opportune time to crack open a Chianti in the spirit of fine Italian food and wine.

2 eggplants

Avocado oil

Sea salt

2 cups (340 g) cooked sorghum

6½ oz (184 g) pesto

½ cup (62 g) ricotta

Zest of 2 lemons

1 cup (40 g) chopped fresh mint

½ cup (76 g) chopped sun-dried tomatoes (in extra virgin olive oil)

Grated Parmesan, to taste

To Serve

Roasted red pepper pesto or bruschetta mix

Slivered almonds

Grated Parmesan

Fresh herbs

Lemon zest

Slice the eggplants lengthwise into ¼-inch (6-mm)-thick slices. Brush each slice with the oil and sprinkle with salt. Heat a grill pan over medium-high heat, and grill the slices until golden and tender, about 3 minutes per side. Arrange the grilled slices on a sheet pan and set aside.

In a mixing bowl, combine the cooked sorghum, pesto, ricotta, lemon zest, fresh mint and sun-dried tomatoes until evenly dispersed. Set aside.

Preheat the oven to 375°F (190°C), and grease a 10-inch (25-cm) cast-iron skillet (or comparable oven-safe dish) with oil.

To assemble the rolls, place 1 to 2 spoonfuls of the filling at the wider end of the eggplant slice and roll up. Place the rolled eggplant in a cast iron skillet, and repeat with the remaining slices. The rolls should be tight together. Sprinkle with the Parmesan cheese, and bake until the cheese is melted, about 15 minutes.

To serve, add a dollop of the red pepper pesto or bruschetta mix, slivered almonds and extra Parmesan. Garnish with fresh herbs of choice and/or lemon zest.

Thai-Inspired Slow Cooker Pork with Cornmeal Sopes

CORNMEAL | MAKES 6–8 SERVINGS

More than a "melting pot," I wish America would adopt "potluck" as its identity. It'd be a grand place where everyone would be invited to share their experiences, to engage with others, to learn and to create something stronger and more beautiful than a menu created by one could ever be. This dish is like a potluck in one. It's a collection of inspiring flavors from different cuisines.

The coveted bao buns at Noodlehead, my favorite Pittsburgh Thai restaurant, inspired the sweet and spicy notes of this slow cooker pork. Think cinnamon, fennel and spicier chili and Sriracha. In lieu of Noodlehead's cloud-like steamed rice bun, this recipe finishes with traditional Mexican sopes. Think of sopes like tacos, but with more substance for sopping up the delicious Thai-inspired sauces. The components may not be 100% authentic, but they are my earnest attempt to be a better observer, a more conscientious eater and to expand my own repertoire, so pull out your slow cooker, and by all means, please add your own twist.

Thai Pork

3 lbs (1.4 kg) pork shoulder (Boston butt), fat trimmed

Salt and pepper, freshly ground

3–4 tbsp (23–30 g) ground dried ginger

4 green onions, diced

8 cloves garlic, diced

½ cup (120 ml) amino acids or gluten-free soy sauce

2 tbsp (29 g) grated fresh ginger

1 tbsp (15 ml) honey

1 tbsp (15 ml) rice vinegar

1 tbsp (15 ml) sesame oil

1 tbsp (10 g) sesame seeds

4 star anise pods

1 tsp cinnamon

1 tsp peppercorns

½ tsp fennel seeds

¼ tsp ground cloves

1 tsp dried chilli flakes or smoked chilli flakes

1 tbsp (15 ml) Sriracha

6 oz (170 g) tomato paste

1 cup (240 ml) ginger beer

Cornmeal Sopes

3 cups (511 g) masa harina

1½ tsp (8 g) salt

2½ cups (592 ml) warm water

To Serve

Pickled vegetables

Chopped green onion

Fresh cilantro

Chopped peanuts or cashews

Hot sauce or Sriracha

(continued)

Thai-Inspired Slow Cooker Pork with Cornmeal Sopes (continued)

To make the Thai pork, rub the pork generously with the salt, pepper and ground ginger, then place in the slow cooker, cover and set aside to marinate for about an hour. Meanwhile, combine all of the remaining ingredients in a mixing bowl, and stir to combine. Transfer the sauce to the slow cooker, cover and cook on low, until cooked and tender, about 8 to 9 hours for a standard slow cooker. Adjust the time accordingly if you're using a clay slow cooker or an Instant Pot. Once the pork is cooked, turn off the slow cooker and allow it to cool. Transfer the meat to a tray and shred it with forks. Pour the sauce over the meat, and reserve excess liquid in the pot for future servings.

To make the sopes, line a sheet pan with parchment paper and set aside. In a mixing bowl, whisk together the masa harina and salt. Stir in the warm water, then knead until the mixture becomes a ball. Divide the dough into 16 portions; shape into balls, arrange on the sheet pan and cover with a damp paper towel and plastic wrap to prevent the dough from drying out. Line a separate sheet pan with parchment paper. Heat a griddle over medium heat.

Working between two sheets of wax paper, use your hands or a rolling pin to press each ball into a 3½-inch (8.9-cm) circle. Cook the dough discs over medium heat for 1 to 2 minutes, or until the bottoms are lightly set. Flip and cook for 2 minutes longer. Remove the sopes from the heat. Quickly and carefully, pinch the edges of the sopes to form a rim. Return the sopes to the griddle to cook until the bottoms are fully set. They should be a lighter brown, but some deeper char marks are okay too. Transfer the sopes to the sheet pan and cover with a tea towel to keep warm and prevent drying. Repeat the process with any remaining dough.

To serve, top each sope with a generous heap of the pulled pork and pickled vegetables. Garnish with chopped green onion, fresh cilantro and chopped nuts. For more heat, add some hot sauce or Sriracha.

> TIPS & TRICKS
> *Be sure to buy masa harina, the traditional tortilla flour made by soaking hominy in limewater (calcium hydroxide—not lime juice). The hominy is then ground into a dough, then dried to create harina, the flour. The limewater adds calcium, as well as changes the structure of the corn, making the nutritionally rich niacin more easily absorbed into the digestive tract. It's the wisdom of centuries!*

Mushroom Bourguignon
with Lemon-Herb Millet

MILLET | VEGETARIAN, VEGAN OPTION | MAKES 4–6 SERVINGS

When New Year's Eve comes around, the Rustbelt Farmer and I like to retreat and hibernate, but that doesn't mean we skip the celebrations. I'll set the table and prepare something that takes a little extra time, a dish that's worth savoring from the end of one year into the blank slate of the next.

One of my favorite traditional dishes to make is boeuf bourguignon. In an effort to extend that celebratory dish to vegetarians, I turned to a variety of mushrooms to create a stew that feels just as festive. The French might scoff, but mushrooms and wine sauce seeping into a lemony herb millet still feels like peasant food at its finest, and I'll toast champagne to that!

Mushroom Bourguignon

2½ tbsp (36 g) unsalted butter, divided

1 tbsp (15 ml) avocado oil

¾ tsp fine sea salt, divided

1¾ lbs (794 g) assorted mushrooms, cleaned and chopped

1 medium yellow onion, diced

1 lb (454 g) carrots, sliced

3 ribs of celery, diced

5 cloves garlic, chopped

¼ cup (62 g) tomato paste

6 sprigs of fresh thyme

2 fresh bay leaves

1 cup (240 ml) port wine

1 cup (240 ml) water

1½ cups (355 ml) vegetable stock

¾ tsp dried thyme

½ tsp ground black pepper

Lemon-Herb Millet

2 tbsp (30 ml) high-heat oil

1 medium onion, small diced

4 cloves garlic, minced

Zest of 1 lemon

2 tsp (10 g) herbs de Provence

1 cup (170 g) millet

1 cup (240 ml) lemon juice

2 cups (480 ml) vegetable stock

¼ tsp salt

2 sprigs fresh rosemary

Sea salt and freshly ground black pepper, to taste

To Serve

Fresh sprigs of thyme and/or tarragon

Grated Parmesan or nutritional yeast

(continued)

Mushroom Bourguignon with Lemon-Herb Millet (continued)

To make the bourguignon, melt half of the butter with 1 tablespoon (15 ml) of oil and ½ teaspoon of salt in a large pot over medium-high heat. Working in batches for more even coverage, add the chopped mushrooms and sauté until brown, reduced in size and have released most of their liquid, about 12 minutes. Strain the liquid, and transfer the mushrooms to a bowl; set aside.

Heat the remaining butter in the pan, and add the diced onion, carrot slices, diced celery and the chopped garlic. Sauté for 8 to 10 minutes, stirring frequently, until the onion has softened and the carrots' color has deepened. Add the tomato paste and cook, stirring for 2 minutes.

Add the thyme (leaves only, not the entire sprigs), bay leaves, port wine and water. Simmer until the wine reduces by about half.

Return the mushrooms to the pot, and add the vegetable stock, dried thyme, pepper and remaining ¼ teaspoon of salt. Bring to a boil, lower the heat and simmer uncovered, stirring occasionally, until the sauce is very thick, about 20 minutes. Remove the bay leaves and discard.

To make the lemon-herb millet, heat the oil in a stockpot or large saucepan over medium-high heat. Add the onion and garlic, and sauté, stirring frequently, until the onion is translucent and tender, about 5 to 7 minutes. Add the lemon zest, herbs de Provence and millet, and continue to cook, until the millet is toasted, about 5 minutes. Add the lemon juice, stock, salt and rosemary sprigs. Increase the heat, and bring to a boil.

Once boiling, reduce the heat to medium-low and simmer until all of the water is absorbed, about 20 to 25 minutes. Season with salt and pepper, to taste.

To serve, place the bourguignon, including any liquid, over the millet. Garnish with fresh sprigs of thyme and/or tarragon and a sprinkle of grated Parmesan cheese (vegetarian) or nutritional yeast (vegan option).

> ### TIPS & TRICKS
> *For the bourguignon, try a meaty mix of mushrooms like maitake, portobello and shiitake. For a completely vegan option, substitute a high-heat oil like avocado oil for the butter.*

Lite Bites & Appetizers

Gussied Up Grains

I'm a "recovering" perfectionist who always has too much on her proverbial plate. When it comes to hosting guests, my eyes are always bigger than my . . . *schedule*. I'll frequently send a message saying, "I'm running just a *tad* behind, so take your time."

When my guests do arrive, appetizers and a glass of wine are ways to entertain while the last minute details of the main course come together. These recipes are nurturing, smoke-and-mirrors ways for you to say, "I'm so glad you're here, but I'm not ready for you just quite yet."

This is a chance for your guests to talk amongst themselves while enjoying beautifully plated, whole-grain bites. Cheeseboards are even more appealing when you tell your guests you made fruit and nut teff crackers from scratch. Teff, which leads the grains in calcium content, also forms a polenta carrier for a restaurant-worthy peach ceviche (Teff Polenta Triangles with Peach Ceviche, page 129).

When used as a flour, teff makes vegan Everything Bagel Crackers (page 138) fit for cheeseboards or afternoon snacking. Millet's creamy texture lends itself to a vegan red pepper dip (Roasted Red Pepper Millet Dip, page 134) whose high magnesium content helps maintain muscle and nerve function. Surrounded by grilled vegetables, it's a spread that can easily become a meal in its own right, but hopefully, your guests won't spoil their appetites because clearly, you have so much more in store!

Teff Polenta Triangles with Peach Ceviche

TEFF | MAKES 6 SERVINGS

For the longest time, I deferred ceviche making to the experts: chefs and my best friend's Ecuadorian family (the *real* experts!). It seemed too complicated to make or too risky (it is raw fish), but as it turns out, ceviche is stupidly simple to make. Paired with a high-protein teff polenta, this combination also *looks* impressive, so even without chef's tweezers, you can plate a restaurant-worthy appetizer that will wow your dinner guests' eyes and most importantly, their taste buds.

Teff Polenta

1½ cups (256 g) teff grain

4 cups (960 ml) low-sodium vegetable stock

1 cup (240 ml) water

1 tsp herbs de Provence

½ tsp garlic powder

Salt and pepper, to taste

1 tbsp (15 g) unsalted butter

Ceviche

½ lb (227 g) fresh halibut, skin removed and cut into ½-inch (13-mm) chunks

1–2 cups (240–480 ml) fresh lime juice

1 small red onion, diced thin

1 cup (161 g) cherry tomatoes, cut in halves or fourths

1 jalapeño, stemmed, seeded and finely chopped

½ cup (20 g) chopped cilantro, plus a few leaves for garnish

1–2 tbsp (15–30 ml) extra virgin olive oil

Pinch of salt

3 tbsp (45 ml) fresh orange juice

1 medium avocado, peeled, pitted and diced

1 peach, pitted and cut into chunks

Lime wedges, for serving

Fresh cilantro, for serving

To make the teff polenta, line an 8 x 8–inch (20 x 20–cm) baking pan with parchment paper and set aside. In a large, heavy-bottom saucepan set over medium-high heat, toast the teff, shaking the pan regularly, until the teff is fragrant and beginning to crackle, 3 to 4 minutes. Add the stock, water, herbs de Provence and garlic powder. Season with salt and pepper to taste. Bring to a boil, lower the heat to medium-low and simmer covered until the mixture is thick and the teff is tender, about 30 minutes. Stir the mixture occasionally, especially toward the end to prevent sticking to the sides and bottom. Remove the saucepan from the heat.

Transfer the teff to the prepared pan. Use an offset spatula or the back of a spoon to evenly distribute the mixture. Let cool to room temperature and then chill for at least 2 hours, but preferably overnight.

To make the ceviche, combine the fish, lime juice and onion in a glass or stainless steel bowl. Use enough lime juice to cover the fish and allow it to float freely. Too little juice will result in unevenly cooked fish. Cover and refrigerate for about 4 hours, until the fish no longer looks raw when broken open (see Tips & Tricks). Drain in a colander.

In a large bowl, mix together the tomatoes, jalapeño, cilantro and olive oil. Stir in the fish and season with salt, usually about ½ teaspoon. Add the orange juice. Cover and refrigerate if not serving immediately. Just before serving, gently stir in the diced avocado and peach chunks.

To serve, use the parchment paper to transfer the chilled teff to a cutting board, and slice into wedges. Heat the butter in a large skillet over medium-high heat. Add the teff wedges, in batches if necessary, and sear for 2 minutes per side, until the edges are lightly browned and crisp. Remove the wedges and transfer to a serving plate. Top each wedge with a scoop of ceviche and serve with a lime wedge and a cilantro garnish.

> ### Tips & Tricks
> *Your best bet is to prepare the polenta the night before your dinner party. This leaves ample time for the teff to set and take shape. For the ceviche, you want to dice the onions as thin as possible, so each little onion bite absorbs a burst of citrus flavor.*
>
> *The fish may be "cooked" in the lime juice a day in advance, but after about 4 hours, when the fish is no longer raw, drain the liquid to prevent the flavor from becoming too tangy and acidic. For the freshest flavor, add the flavorings to the fish no more than a couple of hours before serving.*

Savory Parmesan-Herb Granola

BUCKWHEAT GROATS, ROLLED OATS | VEGETARIAN, VEGAN OPTION | MAKES 10–15 SERVINGS

Armed with an exquisite rhubarb tart from the farmer's market, I sat down at the Sacré-Cœur for a picnic lunch in Montmartre, Paris. Children were enjoying the carousel, beautiful couples were enjoying each other and street performers were enjoying the tips. Everything was perfect as I took my first bite, but as my teeth sank in, I nearly did a spit take. What I assumed was rhubarb was in fact *onion* and though delicious in its own right, it was not at all what I had anticipated.

This savory granola is like that onion tart. In jar form, it might *look* like the standard sweet, breakfast mix of buckwheat groats and rolled oats, but stear clear of the milk. This savory granola is ideal for salty snacking, replacing croutons in salads, or as a salty, crunchy garnish for cheeseboards, especially on creamy varieties like burrata.

Made with lemon zest and herbs, this batch will fill your kitchen with the most heavenly pizza aroma as it bakes. Just be sure to label the jar clearly "SAVORY Granola," lest someone in your family pour milk over the mix and get a rude wake up call before their coffee kicks in. (Or, embrace the trickery and start plotting April Fool's Day? How menacing are you feeling?)

¾ cup (128 g) buckwheat groats

¾ cup (60 g) rolled oats

½ cup (20 g) chopped fresh basil

½ cup (63 g) coarsely chopped pistachios

½ cup (63 g) sunflower seeds

¼ cup (40 g) whole flaxseeds

¼ cup (43 g) flaxseed meal

¼ cup (40 g) raw unsalted pumpkin seeds

2 tbsp (19 g) lemon zest

1 tsp ground turmeric

1 tsp ground thyme

½ tsp sea salt

¼ tsp ground garlic powder

¼ tsp onion powder

Crushed black pepper, to taste

½ cup (120 ml) avocado oil, plus more for greasing

1 tbsp (15 ml) raw honey (use maple syrup for vegan option)

To Serve

Fresh burrata cheese

To make the savory granola, preheat the oven to 350°F (177°C). In a large mixing bowl, stir together the dry ingredients. Pour the the wet ingredients directly onto the dry mixture, and stir to coat evenly.

Grease a 9 x 13–inch (23 x 33–cm) sheet pan with avocado oil. Spread the granola mixture evenly over the pan.

Bake for 15 minutes, then shake and spread into an even layer. Return to the oven, and bake for 15 to 20 minutes more, until crisp. Transfer to a cooling rack and cool completely before storing in an airtight container.

To serve, sprinkle the granola over fresh burrata as part of a cheeseboard, or place a jarful with your spread and let guests serve themselves.

> TIPS & TRICKS
> *This recipe will make a big batch, more than you'll need for one cheese tray, but it makes a healthy substitute for chips or pretzels, so keep some by your work station and keep on crunching.*

Golden Raisin Crackers

Teff | Vegetarian | Makes about 30 crackers

If you really want to impress your dinner guests, casually mention the crackers on your cheeseboard are homemade. It's a process that can start the day before the party, leaving you plenty of time to focus on day-of elements, but the extra attention to detail will make your guests feel extra special.

This recipe starts with a loaf of the Griddled Golden Raisin Bread (page 42). Slicing and baking it a second time yields a wholesome, fancy cracker that will steal the cheeseboard show. Nutty and sweet, these crackers pair especially well with creamy cheeses like chevre or brie, with fresh fruit and herb accents, or a really stinky cheese like morbier. For meat pairings, try a rosemary roasted ham or salty cured meats like a smoky speck, and don't forget the wine!

1 loaf Griddled Golden Raisin Bread (page 42)

TIPS & TRICKS
Double this recipe, and save one loaf for breakfast, or freeze the second loaf for making more crackers down the line.

To make the crackers, wrap the loaf in plastic wrap or foil. Place in the freezer for at least 2 hours. You want the bread to be frozen and firm enough to slice it thinly, but not a frozen brick. If you're in a rush, you can skip the freezing. Thin slices will be just a bit trickier.

Preheat the oven to 400°F (204°C). Line two sheet pans with parchment paper.

Remove the bread from the freezer. Let sit 10 minutes to thaw slightly.

With a serrated knife, cut the bread into ⅛-inch (3-mm) slices. The slices should be as uniform as possible. Arrange the slices on the pans without any overlap.

Bake for 8 to 10 minutes until the crackers are a deep golden brown and corners start to crisp. Let cool completely before serving. Store the crackers in an airtight container.

Roasted Red Pepper Millet Dip

MILLET | VEGAN | MAKES 2 CUPS (491 G)

There are lots of methods to create vegan dips these days, but a lot of them involve soaking nuts for extended periods of time. By blending cooked millet, an ancient grain from the Far East, with roasted red peppers, this recipe creates a creamy, nut-free, vegan dip with minimal effort and extra fiber and magnesium. Paired with an explosion of grilled vegetables and crudites, this is an appetizer that could easily become a meal in its own right.

1 tbsp (15 ml) avocado oil

6 large cloves garlic, coarsely chopped

1 cup (170 g) cooked millet

1 cup (170 g) chopped roasted red pepper

¼ cup (38 g) nutritional yeast

1 tsp smoked paprika

½ cup (76 g) chopped sun-dried tomatoes (drained from oil)

Sea salt and black pepper

To Serve

Drizzle of oil

Roasted chickpeas or toasted sorghum

Fresh herbs, to garnish

Grilled vegetables, for dipping

To make the dip, heat the oil in a small saucepan over medium heat. Add the garlic and sauté until lightly browned and fragrant. Remove from the heat. Strain the garlic from any remaining oil, and transfer to a food processor or blender. Add the cooked millet, chopped roasted red pepper, nutritional yeast and smoked paprika, and pulse until combined. Add the chopped sun-dried tomatoes, and pulse until well mixed but some chunks remain. Season generously with sea salt and black pepper.

TIPS & TRICKS
Nutritional yeast is a terrible sounding name for a naturally derived, nutrition-packed flake that tastes like Parmesan cheese. You can usually find it at salad bars in natural grocery stores if you want to take a test drive before you buy.

Crispy Sweet Potato "Sliders" with Quinoa-Curry Chicken Salad

QUINOA | MAKES ABOUT 30 SWEET POTATO SLIDERS, 10–15 SERVINGS

When my oldest sister was a grad student at the University of Nebraska, I would count down the days until our visit for two reasons: 1. I loved and missed my sister immensely, and 2. I loved and missed the chicken salad from her local grocery store immensely. I was a mere first grader, so I doubt the chicken salad was very refined, but it still holds a fond place in my heart (as does my sister, for the record). This Quinoa-Curry Chicken Salad is elevated casual. It's a creamy, comforting deli staple with some new spices and healthier twists. Dolloped onto crispy sweet potatoes, this appetizer is a lowbrow delight!

Curry Chicken

1 lb (454 g) skinless boneless chicken tenderloins or chicken breasts cut in half horizontally

Tandoori masala seasoning or curry powder

Garlic powder

Onion powder

Salt and pepper

Spray oil, such as coconut oil

Sweet Potatoes

1¼ lb (567 g) sweet potato

2 tbsp (22 g) potato starch or cornstarch

2 tsp (10 g) tandoori masala seasoning

½ tsp kosher salt

3 tbsp (45 ml) avocado oil

Chicken Salad

1 cup (170 g) cooked quinoa

½ cup (58 g) toasted walnuts, chopped

2 ribs of celery, chopped

2 tbsp (20 g) sunflower seeds

½ cup (76 g) red grapes, quartered

¼ cup (10 g) chopped cilantro

1½ cups (368 g) Greek yogurt

1 tbsp (8 g) tandoori masala seasoning or curry powder

Salt and pepper, to taste

Whole cilantro leaves, to serve

To make the curry chicken, pat the chicken dry with paper towels, then sprinkle with an even coating of tandoori masala, garlic powder and onion powder. Season with salt and pepper, then spray with the coconut oil. Heat a grill pan or a nonstick skillet over medium-high heat. Sauté the chicken until golden brown and cooked through, about 10 to 12 minutes, flipping periodically. Transfer the chicken to a cutting board to cool, then chop into small chunks. Store in the fridge until ready to mix the salad.

To make the sweet potatoes, arrange a rack in the middle of the oven and heat to 400°F (204°C). Cut the sweet potato into ¼-inch (6-mm)-thick rings (cut the rings on a slight angle for a fancier appetizer presentation). Place the sweet potato slices in a large mixing bowl. Add the potato starch or cornstarch. Tossing the sweet potatoes with the starch helps absorb the potato's moisture and creates a crispier texture than regular roasting. Add the tandoori seasoning and salt. Shake to combine, and use a spatula to collect any dry mix that falls to the bottom of the bowl. Add the oil, and toss vigorously to coat.

Spread the coated sweet potato slices in a single layer on an ungreased baking sheet. Roast for 15 minutes. Flip the sweet potatoes and continue to roast until the potatoes are tender on the inside and crispy on the outside, 30 to 35 minutes more. In the meantime, start to prepare the quinoa. Once the sweet potatoes are done, remove from the oven, sprinkle with additional salt and set aside.

To make the chicken salad, spread the cooked quinoa in an even layer on a baking sheet. Bake at 400°F (204°C) for 15 minutes to toast. Remove from the oven and let cool slightly. You can toast the walnuts whole at this point, too. Just position them separately on the pan, and keep an eye on them because they'll toast faster than the quinoa. Transfer the quinoa and toasted walnuts to a medium mixing bowl. Add the curry chicken, celery, sunflower seeds, red grapes, cilantro, yogurt and the tandoori seasoning, and stir to combine. Season with salt and pepper to taste.

To serve, add a dollop of chicken salad to each sweet potato slice and top with a fresh cilantro sprig to garnish.

> TIPS & TRICKS
> *If you have extra chicken salad, roll it in a lettuce or collard wrap, and pack it for lunch.*

Everything Bagel Crackers

TEFF FLOUR │ VEGAN │ MAKES ABOUT 35 (1½-INCH [3.8-CM]) CRACKERS

One of our favorite ways to eat dinner is to load up a cutting board with crackers, cheeses and raw veggies, and settle into a glass of wine and a good movie. These are crackers for more casual times. They're hearty, salty and extremely snackable, but you can still dress them up and take them to nice places too. Bringing a cheese plate with homemade crackers to a dinner party is a surefire way to impress.

½ cup (85 g) teff flour

¾ cup (72 g) almond flour

3 tbsp (18 g) everything bagel seasoning blend

2 tbsp (11 g) ground flaxseed

1 tbsp nutritional yeast

½ tsp dried ground thyme

¼ tsp baking soda

¼ cup (60 ml) water

1 tbsp (15 ml) avocado oil or olive oil

Preheat the oven to 350°F (177°C) and line a baking sheet with parchment paper.

Sift the teff flour and almond flour into a large mixing bowl. Add the everything bagel seasoning, ground flaxseed, nutritional yeast, ground thyme and baking soda, and whisk to combine.

Add the water and oil and mix well. Use your hands to knead the mixture together until it becomes a dough. If it's too dry, add a drizzle of oil. Shape the dough into a ball, and transfer to the parchment paper–lined pan.

Use a rolling pin to roll out the dough until it's about ⅛ inch (3 mm) thick, or as thin as you can get it without tearing. With a pastry wheel or a pizza slicer, divide the dough into crackers.

Bake the crackers for 18 to 20 minutes until slightly golden and crisp. If you want a really salty cracker, brush with oil and sprinkle with salt after removing from the oven. Cool on a baking sheet for 10 minutes. Store in an airtight container once cooled.

Soups & Stews

Creamy Grains

From a big pot of soup simmering on the stovetop to a chilled summer bowl, soups have the ability to nourish and comfort us. Serve these as a light first course, a hearty main or initiate a soup swap to keep the warm bowls flowing.

The textures of the tinier grains—amaranth and teff—really shine in the Creamy Amaranth Corn Chowder (page 146), Smoky Cream of Tomato Soup (page 144) and the Teff Ethiopian-Style Stew (page 148). They add the hearty creaminess you'd expect from dairy, without the use of butter or cream, so these soups remain vegan without adding any soy, fake or processed ingredients.

Tiny but mighty teff not only thickens these soups, but it is high in iron, which aids in circulation and prevents fatigue. Women and those following vegetarian or vegan diets are especially at risk for iron deficiency, so get that stockpot out and start eating some stew! All these recipes freeze well too, so your freezer can become a gift that keeps on giving.

Fall Harvest Soup with Quinoa & Crispy Sage

QUINOA | VEGAN | MAKES 4 SERVINGS

Come September, the return of crossing guards, bus stops, flashing school zones and the *sea* of children pouring from yellow buses leaves me relishing my age. Middle school can stay lodged in my past. Back then, fall mainly represented a return to disgruntled teachers, gym class uniforms, gym class locker rooms, just the horror of gym class in general, and airtight buildings that I swear gave me allergies.

Fall as a kid is bittersweet, but fall as an adult is cozy, comforting and full of choices—should I drink spiked hot apple cider and watch Netflix, or should I drink red wine and watch Amazon Prime (#LiveItUp)? These days, I am all too willing to break out the blankets and embrace fall at the slightest hint of a chill. Cupping a bowl of warm, creamy soup while donning my well worn middle school athletics sweatshirt is the best of adulthood: It's the epitome of fall in each cinnamon-spiced spoonful.

Soup

1 tbsp (15 g) coconut oil
½ cup (76 g) chopped onion
1 tsp minced garlic
½ cup (85 g) quinoa, rinsed
3½ cups (828 ml) vegetable stock
3 cups (540 g) diced sweet potato
2 cups (510 g) unsweetened applesauce
¼ cup (60 ml) maple syrup
¼ cup (10 g) chopped sage
½ tsp ground cinnamon, plus additional for garnish
½ tsp ground ginger
½ tsp ground turmeric
¼ tsp salt
1 (13.5-oz [382-g]) can full-fat coconut milk (with cream on top)

Crispy Sage

¼ cup (55 g) coconut oil
¾ oz (21 g) fresh sage
Sea salt

To make the soup, heat the coconut oil in a 3-quart (2.8-L) saucepan over medium heat. Add the chopped onion and garlic, cooking until the onions are softened, about 5 to 7 minutes. Add the rinsed quinoa, stirring frequently, until fragrant and toasted, about 3 to 5 minutes.

Add the stock, sweet potatoes, applesauce, maple syrup, chopped sage, cinnamon, ginger, turmeric and salt. Bring to a boil, then reduce to a simmer. Cover and cook until the quinoa and sweet potatoes are cooked, about 15 to 18 minutes, until the quinoa grains appear to be sprouted and are translucent around the edges. Allow the soup to cool slightly. Stir in the coconut milk and the coconut cream into the soup. Process the soup in batches in a blender or food processor, until smooth and creamy. Return the soup to the saucepan and keep warm while you prepare the crispy sage.

To make the crispy sage, heat the oil in a small skillet over medium-high heat until hot. Add the sage leaves to the oil, and fry until crisp, 10 to 15 seconds. Gently transfer with a fork to paper towels and sprinkle generously with coarse salt. Serve the soup warm with a crispy sage garnish.

> ### TIPS & TRICKS
> *Want something to dip into this creamy soup? Try dried pears or apple slices, or homemade Golden Raisin Crackers (page 133).*

Smoky Cream of Tomato Soup

Amaranth | Vegan | Makes 10 servings

Tomato soup takes me back to Saturday afternoons as a kid, heating myself a can of soup, begging for a grilled cheese, then watching *Hook* on repeat until the VHS mysteriously disappeared (did my sisters sabotage me?). Perhaps, it was Rufio's feasts that inspired my journey into food and entertaining later in life?

The creaminess of this tomato soup comes from blending the amaranth, so it's a vegan soup option with high protein and calcium, key nutrients for a vegan diet. The smoked paprika and fire-roasted tomatoes add a noticeable smoky flavor, so it's a far cry from the sugar-laden cans of my childhood. This soup is all the nostalgia and none of the corn syrup. For a more complete visit to childhood, save some Cheddar-Jalapeño Waffles (page 58) from brunch to dip into your soup and rewatch *Hook*. That movie really holds up!

2 tbsp (30 ml) avocado oil

4 ribs of celery, chopped

1 large yellow onion, diced

3 cloves garlic, minced

2 tbsp (15 g) smoked paprika

2 red bell peppers, chopped

1 cup (170 g) dry amaranth

4 cups (960 ml) vegetable stock

2 (28-oz [794-g]) cans fire-roasted crushed tomatoes

2 cups (402 g) no-salt-added cooked cannellini beans or Great Northern white beans, rinsed and drained, divided

1 cup (180 g) diced carrots

1 tsp (5 g) salt

To Serve

Herb-infused olive oil

1–2 tbsp (3–5 g) fresh herbs such as basil or thyme

In a large saucepan, heat the avocado oil over medium-low heat. Add the chopped celery, diced onion, minced garlic and smoked paprika, stirring occasionally, until the vegetables start to soften, about 10 minutes. Add the chopped red pepper, dry amaranth and vegetable stock. Bring to a boil.

Add the fire-roasted crushed tomatoes, 1 cup (201 g) of cannellini beans, diced carrots and salt. Reduce the heat and simmer for 40 to 45 minutes, until the carrots are soft and the amaranth is fully cooked. The amaranth will look translucent on its edges when it's fully cooked.

Remove from the heat. Use an immersion blender, a food processor or a blender to blend the mixture until creamy.

Return to the heat, and stir in the remaining cannellini beans. Ladle into bowls, drizzle with infused olive oil, garnish with fresh herbs and enjoy!

> **TIPS & TRICKS**
> *This makes a big batch of soup, and it freezes well, so you can save some for the future.*

Creamy Amaranth Corn Chowder

AMARANTH │ VEGAN │ MAKES 10 SERVINGS

From my grandparents' sprawling farm in South Dakota to my parents' garden, corn came to symbolize my roots. But corn, specifically corn *syrup*, grew to symbolize industrialized food systems and a loss of trustworthy food sources. When I find *true* corn, sweet, imperfect corn from smaller farmers, who have resisted industrial farming practices, all I want to do is celebrate. This is a celebration soup!

The creamy texture of this vegan chowder comes from blending amaranth instead of dairy. Amaranth packs all the essential amino acids, including lysine, which is lacking in most grains. Plus, organic, non-GMO corn (available frozen from several organic sources if you can't find it locally) is linked to two antioxidants attributed to eye and skin health called zeaxanthin and lutein, so you can celebrate your health, too.

2 tbsp (30 ml) avocado oil

2 ribs of celery, chopped

1 yellow onion, diced

1 red or yellow bell pepper, chopped

2 cloves garlic, minced

1 cup (170 g) dry amaranth

4 cups (960 ml) vegetable stock

4 cups (960 ml) filtered water

4 cups (577 g) corn kernels, divided

1 cup (180 g) diced carrots

1 cup (180 g) diced, peeled sweet potato

1 tsp salt

1–2 tbsp (3–5 g) fresh chopped French tarragon, for serving

In a large saucepan, heat the avocado oil over low heat. Add the chopped celery, diced onion, chopped pepper and minced garlic, stirring occasionally, until the vegetables start to soften, about 10 minutes.

Add the dry amaranth, vegetable stock and water. Bring to a boil.

Add 2 cups (289 g) of the corn kernels, the carrots, sweet potato and salt. Reduce the heat and simmer for 40 to 45 minutes, until the sweet potatoes are soft and the amaranth is fully cooked (it will look partially translucent, like quinoa, only smaller).

Remove from the heat, and use an immersion blender, a food processor or a blender to blend the mixture until creamy.

Return to the heat, and stir in the remaining corn kernels. Ladle into bowls, garnish with tarragon and enjoy!

TIPS & TRICKS

Change up your garnishes as you work through leftovers of this soup. Fresh tarragon or dill, crispy pan-fried shallots and/or garlic, toasted almonds or roasted corn all complement this creamy corn soup well. If dairy-free is not a concern, top with a dollop of Greek yogurt for a tangy, probiotic-rich garnish.

Teff Ethiopian-Style Stew

TEFF | VEGAN | MAKES 6–8 SERVINGS

While on an architectural field trip in Washington, D.C., our professors released us into the night with a lot of trust and a few key pieces of advice, mainly "Go to Little Ethiopia and try Ethiopian cuisine!" That we did! Sandra, Nina and I shared a meal, not just proverbially. We used our hands and the spongy injera bread (made from teff) to scoop up the slow-cooked saucy stews from one large plate. The bond we formed that night has endured, grown and changed since then, and in the process, we've regrouped to celebrate several occasions over platters of injera and stews.

Teff, Ethiopia's ancient grain, gives this stew a hearty creaminess, but the secret is the spice mixture—sweet, warming and just a tad spicy. It may sound cheesy, but when that allspice hits the pan, take a minute to inhale it deeply. It's such a warming, comforting blend and a reminder to enjoy the process, not just scurry to achieve the outcome.

2 tbsp (28 g) coconut oil

2 cups (303 g) chopped onion

4 cloves garlic, minced

½ tsp smoked paprika

½ tsp dried harissa seasoning

½ tsp ground cinnamon

½ tsp ground allspice

¼ tsp cayenne pepper

½ tsp sea salt

1 cup (170 g) uncooked teff

4 cups (960 ml) unsalted vegetable stock

1 cup (240 ml) water

3 cups (540 g) peeled and cubed sweet potatoes

2 red bell peppers, chopped

1 (14.5-oz [411-g]) can fire-roasted crushed tomatoes

3 cups (540 g) chopped zucchini

2 (15-oz [425-g]) cans garbanzo beans, rinsed

⅓ cup (60 g) creamy peanut butter

¼ cup (60 ml) lemon juice

1½ tsp (8 g) kosher salt

Fresh herbs, to garnish

Lemon wedges, to serve

Heat a large pot over medium heat. Add the oil to the pan; swirl to coat.

Add the onion and cook until soft, about 5 minutes. Add the garlic, paprika, harissa, cinnamon, allspice, cayenne pepper and salt and let cook, stirring constantly, for about 1 minute. Add the teff and cook, stirring constantly for 2 minutes.

Add the stock, water, sweet potatoes, red bell peppers and the crushed tomatoes, and bring to a boil. Cover, reduce the heat and simmer for 20 minutes, stirring occasionally.

Add the zucchini, and give the mix a good stir. Cover and simmer 10 minutes, or until the zucchini and the sweet potatoes are tender.

Add the garbanzo beans, peanut butter, lemon juice and salt. Let the garbanzo beans warm through, 3 to 4 minutes.

To serve, ladle into bowls, garnish with fresh herbs such as rosemary or cilantro and serve with a lemon wedge.

> TIPS & TRICKS
> *This makes a big pot, so to add variety to leftovers, try serving this in an acorn squash roasted with similar spices as the stew.*

Chilled Rhubarb-Radish Soup with Mint Vinaigrette

Rolled Oats, Buckwheat Groats | *Vegetarian* | *Makes 8 servings*

"You want that? That weedy thing? I was going to weed whack it." This was a typical conversation between neighbors and my mom, who salvaged many a rhubarb plant from unknowing neighbors (to be fair, this was *long* before Pinterest blew up with rhubarb recipes). I would watch in delightful anticipation of the sweet wonders that would soon be emerging from my mom's oven, which I'm sure she graciously shared with the neighbors.

This chilled soup recipe celebrates rhubarb season with a bit of a twist—though slightly sweet and fruity, this recipe pushes rhubarb to the savory side of the menu. It's a refreshing start to a summer gathering, especially when drizzled with mint vinaigrette. The same Rose-Colored Roasted Beet & Rose Water Granola (page 34) you eat for breakfast complements the color and texture of this creamy soup. If you want to get real fancy, dish this soup in small glasses and serve as shooters at your next spring or summer soirée.

Radish Soup

5 (1 lb [454 g]) stalks rhubarb, chopped

1 bunch (10–12) radishes, quartered

1 inch (3 cm) chunk of fresh ginger, peeled and diced

2½ cups (592 ml) water

1 lb (454 g) strawberries, quartered

1 cup (40 g) chopped fresh mint

3 tbsp (45 ml) balsamic vinegar

Sea salt, to taste

Mint Vinaigrette

¼ cup (10 g) chopped fresh mint

Juice of 1 lemon

⅓ cup (78 ml) extra virgin olive oil

2 tbsp (30 ml) white wine vinegar

1 tsp (5 ml) honey

Sea salt, to taste

To Serve

Rose-Colored Roasted Beet & Rose Water Granola (page 34)

Greek yogurt

To make the soup, add the rhubarb, radishes, ginger and water to a wide-mouthed saucepan. Bring to a boil, then turn down the heat and let simmer until the rhubarb and radishes are tender, around 5 to 8 minutes. Remove from the heat, and let cool slightly. Then transfer to a food processor or a blender. Add the strawberries, fresh mint and balsamic vinegar, and purée. Salt to taste.

To make the mint vinaigrette, combine the mint and lemon juice in a small saucepan. Bring to a boil and remove from the heat. Let steep for about 10 minutes. Strain into a large bowl, pressing on the leaves to extract all the liquid. You should have about 3 tablespoons (45 ml) of liquid after straining. Add the oil, vinegar and honey; whisk until well combined. Salt to taste.

To serve, garnish with Rose-Colored Roasted Beet & Rose Water Granola, a dollop of thick and creamy Greek yogurt and a drizzle of mint vinaigrette.

Sides & Salads
A Grainy Crunch

If you find yourself asking, "What can I bring?" these sides and salads are your answer. A loaf of Lemon & Thyme Quick Bread (page 154), made with nutty and buttery millet flour, pairs well with lighter meals and its leftovers can be used to make a homemade crouton (Brown Butter Lemon & Thyme Croutons, page 157).

These seasonal salads are more unexpected than your average assortment of vegetables, and crunchier grains like sorghum and al dente buckwheat make great conversation starters too. You get to play the grain tour guide, explaining the history and health benefits of these lesser known grains.

Lemon & Thyme Quick Bread

MILLET FLOUR | VEGETARIAN | MAKES 1 (8 X 4 X 2–INCH [20 X 10 X 5–CM]) LOAF

Millet flour adds a nutty and buttery flavor to baking, and the almond flour, which is high in healthy fats, adds moisture to this bread recipe. The difference between almond flour and meal is the coarseness of the grind, with almond flour being finer. For recipes like this quick bread, the two are interchangeable.

The resulting bread is sweet enough to grab for a wholesome breakfast-on-the-go, but the lemon and thyme make this slice a complement to fresh salads and lighter dinners too. Plus, you can turn leftovers into croutons (page 157).

Melted butter or coconut oil, for greasing

½ cup (120 ml) milk or cream

Finely grated zest and juice of 1 lemon

1 cup (130 g) millet flour

1 cup (96 g) almond flour/meal

½ cup (96 g) coconut sugar or raw cane sugar

1½ tsp (6 g) baking powder

½ tsp baking soda

½ tsp sea salt

1 tbsp (3 g) fresh thyme

1 tsp dried herbs de Provence

¾ cup (177 ml) extra virgin olive oil, plus more for pan

3 large eggs, room temperature

Preheat the oven to 325°F (165°C). Grease a 8 x 4 x 2–inch (20 x 10 x 5–cm) loaf pan with melted butter or coconut oil, and line with parchment paper. Set aside.

Combine the milk and lemon juice in a bowl, and let stand until thickened, about 5 minutes.

Sift the millet flour, almond flour, coconut sugar, baking powder, baking soda and salt into a mixing bowl, and whisk to combine. Stir in the lemon zest, thyme and herbs de Provence.

In the bowl of a standing mixer, beat the lemon-milk mixture, olive oil and eggs, until combined. Pour the liquid mix over the dry mix. Stir to combine.

Pour the batter into the loaf pan. Bake until the bread is golden and a tester inserted in center comes out clean, about 55 minutes. Let cool completely in pan on a wire rack.

> TIPS & TRICKS
> *Once you've made this bread, try it again with a different herb combination.*

Brown Butter Lemon & Thyme Croutons

MILLET FLOUR | VEGETARIAN | MAKES 4 CUPS (682 G)

The simplest of salads will elevate with the inclusion of these Brown Butter Lemon & Thyme Croutons, and you can pat yourself on the back because rather than tossing leftover bread, you're repurposing it into a versatile ingredient!

4 cups (682 g) cubed day-old Lemon & Thyme Quick Bread (page 154), cut in ½-inch (13-mm) cubes (about half a loaf)

½ cup (115 g) salted butter

2 shallots, minced

2 tbsp (5 g) fresh thyme leaves

½ cup (90 g) fine grated Parmesan or pecorino, optional

Preheat the oven to 350°F (177°C).

Spread the bread cubes evenly on a baking sheet and bake until browned and crispy, about 15 to 20 minutes.

Cook the butter, stirring constantly, in a saucepan over medium heat until foaming, about 5 minutes. Swirl the pan to prevent uneven cooking, and cook until the butter becomes golden tan, about 30 to 60 seconds more. Add the shallots, and cook until the shallots are translucent and tender. Add the thyme and cook, stirring often, 1 minute.

Drizzle the butter mixture over the toasted bread and toss with the cheese, if using.

Roasted Squash & Grape Salad
with Bacon & Burnt Honey Vinaigrette

MILLET FLOUR | VEGETARIAN & VEGAN OPTIONS | MAKES 6 SERVINGS

For most of the year, this dish would be considered an *entrée*. Or, pair the salad components with quinoa, grilled chicken or fish, and you have yourself a grain bowl. However, when it comes to holidays, this is a hearty, sweet and savory "side dish" that will have you winning friends and influencing people without the need for ol' Dale Carnegie.

For a variation on this side, swap Parmesan Quinoa Crisps (page 82) for the croutons. If you're bringing this salad to a family gathering or holiday feast, go the extra mile and make a little "gluten-free" tag for your dish, so gluten-free eaters know they have the green light.

Roasted Squash

16 oz (454 g) Brussels sprouts, halved

1 large acorn squash, cut into wedges

3 cups (16 oz [454 g]) seedless red grapes

3 shallots, peeled and halved

2 tbsp (5 g) fresh thyme

2 tbsp (5 g) chopped sage

2 tbsp (30 ml) avocado oil

2 tbsp (30 ml) unsalted butter, melted

Salt and pepper, to taste

4 pieces thick-cut bacon, chopped, optional

Vinaigrette

½ cup (120 ml) honey

⅔ cup (156 ml) apple cider vinegar

2 tbsp (25 g) finely chopped shallot

1 tbsp (15 ml) Dijon mustard

1 tsp salt

½ tsp black pepper

⅔ cup (156 ml) olive oil

To Serve

Brown Butter Lemon & Thyme Croutons (page 157)

Arugula

Slivered almonds

Fresh thyme

Lemon zest

To make the roasted squash, preheat the oven to 425°F (220°C). Combine the Brussels sprouts, acorn squash wedges, grapes, shallots, thyme and sage in a large bowl. Drizzle with the oil and melted butter, and season generously with salt and pepper. Toss to coat. Spread the mixture evenly on a large rimmed baking sheet. Roast the mixture for 30 minutes, then remove from the oven, add the chopped bacon and toss. Continue to roast until the squash and onion begin to brown, stirring occasionally, 20 to 30 minutes. Meanwhile, prepare the vinaigrette.

To make the vinaigrette, heat a skillet over medium-high heat. Add the honey, and cook until it is dark amber in color and smells caramelized, about 2 minutes, swirling the pan and scraping down the sides. Remove from the heat and immediately whisk in the vinegar. Whisk in the chopped shallot, mustard, salt and pepper. Slowly whisk in the oil until combined.

To serve, transfer the roasted mixture to a platter and toss with Lemon & Thyme Croutons and arugula, if using. Sprinkle with slivered almonds, fresh thyme and lemon zest. Serve with the vinaigrette on the side.

> **TIPS & TRICKS**
> *For a vegetarian option, skip the bacon. To make this a vegan option, omit the bacon, skip the butter and double the oil. To make this a cheese lover's dish, add shaved Parmesan.*

Watermelon-Sorghum Salad with Blackberry Vinaigrette

SORGHUM | VEGETARIAN, VEGAN OPTION | MAKES 7–10 SERVINGS

Salad meets salsa, meets the best of summer entertaining with this refreshing watermelon and sorghum combination. Serve this dish as a side for Quinoa "Fish" Fritter Tacos (page 93). As an added perk, with the ingredients you'll have on hand to make this salad, you'll also have cocktail options! You'll be well equipped to top off that meal with blackberry-jalapeño margaritas, or freeze watermelon cubes and chill a white wine sangria with extra flavor and color.

Sorghum Salad

4 cups (606 g) scooped or chopped seeded watermelon

1 cucumber, quartered and sliced

1 small red onion, chopped

1 jalapeño pepper, seeded and diced

½ cup (20 g) fresh basil leaves, finely chopped

⅔ cup (27 g) chopped fresh cilantro leaves

½ cup (20 g) chopped fresh mint

Zest and juice of 3 limes

2 cups (170 g) cooked sorghum

Sea salt and freshly ground pepper, to taste

Blackberry Vinaigrette

1 cup (151 g) ripe blackberries

1 tbsp (15 ml) honey (use maple syrup for vegan option)

3 tbsp (45 ml) pomegranate or balsamic vinegar

2 tbsp (30 ml) olive oil

Zest and juice of 1 lime

1 tsp Dijon mustard

½ tsp salt

To make the salad, toss all of the ingredients together until combined. Serve immediately, or cover and refrigerate for up to 2 days.

To make the dressing, combine all of the ingredients in a small blender or food processor, and blend until creamy.

> TIPS & TRICKS
> *Remember to cook the sorghum ahead of time, since it takes about an hour, or better yet, plan to make this dish during a week when you're using sorghum as a base for your grain bowls and have some grains to spare.*

Summary Harvest Salad with Crunchy Buckwheat

BUCKWHEAT | VEGETARIAN, VEGAN OPTION | MAKES 4–6 SERVINGS

This is a salad for the heart of summer, when you still want to gather with friends, but turning on the oven feels like torture. It's a foolproof recipe, too. Even if you're heavy-handed on one component, it will still be a refreshing hit with your guests, especially if you're sitting outside drinking an extra chilled bottle of wine.

The al-dente buckwheat adds a crunchy accent, but it also adds zinc, copper and manganese to your diet. These help bolster the immune system, which is helpful no matter the season. Want to destress your plans even more? While you have the grill fired up, cook some chicken or salmon, bulk up the greens and this salad can easily become the main course.

Summer Harvest Salad

1¾ cups (414 ml) water

1 cup (170 g) buckwheat

4 ears (3 cups [433 g]) of corn

3 firm peaches or nectarines

1–2 tbsp (15–30 ml) melted coconut oil

2 cups (303 g) blueberries

1 cup (40 g) chopped fresh mint

1 cup (40 g) chopped fresh parsley

1 cup (40 g) chopped fresh basil

Mixed greens, to serve

Strawberry Chia Dressing

8 oz (227 g) strawberries, hulled

¼ cup (60 ml) olive oil

3 tbsp (45 ml) white wine vinegar

2 tsp (10 ml) honey (use maple syrup for vegan option)

1 tsp Dijon style mustard

2 tbsp (20 g) chia seeds

To make the buckwheat, bring the water and buckwheat to a boil in a medium saucepan. Remove from the heat. Cover and let stand 10 minutes, or until most of the liquid is absorbed and the buckwheat is soft and chewy. Drain off any excess liquid.

To make the grilled components, you can fire up the grill or use a grill pan over medium-high heat. Shuck and clean the corn. Don't worry about getting every last stray piece of silk—they'll burn away on the grill anyway. Cut the peaches or nectarines in half (you can cut them in slices if using a grill pan) and brush with the melted coconut oil. Place the corn and peach/nectarine halves directly over a very hot fire or grill pan, and grill, turning occasionally, until charred and cooked through, about 4 to 5 minutes for peaches, and 10 minutes for corn. Cut the corn kernels from the cob.

To assemble, toss together the grilled corn kernels, peaches, blueberries, mint, parsley, basil and cooked buckwheat in a large bowl. You can either add the mixed greens to the bowl, or add mixed greens directly to serving bowls, then top with the fruit and grain mixture (this option makes for better leftovers—less wilted greens). Serve with strawberry chia dressing.

To make the dressing, combine strawberries, oil, vinegar, honey and mustard in a blender or food processor. Cover and blend or process until smooth. Add more oil or a little water for a thinner texture. Stir in the chia seeds right before serving. The chia seeds will thicken after sitting.

Dessert

Don't Go To Bed Salty

Dessert is where my kitchen adventures and eventually, my blog, began. My stubborn sweet tooth demanded to be appeased, but my rational brain objected to the processed sugars and preservatives in most desserts. Even the organic desserts left me wanting. Why couldn't there be a whole-grain cake or cookie? Why couldn't there be a higher fiber and protein element to dessert?

Through my baking experiments, I discovered there *could* be crowd-pleasing whole grain desserts, and by extension, there can be crowd-pleasing *gluten-free*, whole-grain desserts. There can be chocolate and cheesecake swirls reminiscent of grade-school cupcakes (Black & Gold Cheesecake Bars, page 166). There can be decadent layer cakes with sweet apple cider drizzles (Apple Season Layer Cake, page 175). There can be protein-packed chocolate truffles for when you just need a *little* something sweet (Dark Chocolate Truffles, page 169).

Quick Tips & Tricks Before You Start Baking

Using whole-grain, gluten-free flours is far from a sacrifice. In addition to the increased health benefits, whole grain flours add sweet, nutty, toasted notes to desserts, richer colors and a heartier bite. They say "never go to bed angry," but I say, "don't go to bed salty." Each day deserves a little sweet celebration, especially when that celebration is made from whole-grain ingredients.

Expect A Different Dessert

As much as I live my life to appease my sweet tooth, I have trained it not to crave the overly sweetened desserts. The combination of healthier whole grains and unrefined sweeteners make for more justifiable desserts that you can actually enjoy without that immediate sugar-rush sick feeling. But these flavors might take some acclimating, so give yourself some time and approach these recipes with an open mind.

How to Measure Gluten-Free Flours

I always joke I am of the "Grandmother school of thought" when it comes to measuring—use what you got, use your eyeballs and *usually*, it's good enough. However, with gluten-free flours, how you measure them can have a big impact on your baking. The best bet is to pour flour into a large mixing bowl, then lightly spoon flour into the designated measuring cup. Spoon more than you'll need, then, working over the bowl, use a butter knife or the spoon handle to level the flour. Return any excess flour to the bag.

Is Baking Powder Gluten-Free?

Baking powder is made from baking soda, cream of tartar (a by-product of wine production) and a "moisture absorption agent" which is usually, but not always, cornstarch. Occasionally, a baking powder will use potato starch (gluten-free), or wheat starch (contains gluten), so baking powder varies from brand to brand. Be sure to read the labels, but as a safe start, popular brands Rumford and Clabber Girl are both gluten free.

Black & Gold Cheesecake Bars

SORGHUM FLOUR | MAKES 1 (9 x 13–INCH [23 x 33–CM]) PAN OF BARS

Chocolate and cheesecake swirls take me back to elementary school, when my mom would ask me what I wanted to bring to school to celebrate my birthday. Year after year, my answer was the same—self-filled cupcakes! As an adult who can now bake for herself, I still find myself returning January after January to that winning combination, but the cream cheese has become a blank canvas for my experimentation.

This version is rooted in a dorky play on words: black and gold, an ode to Pittsburgh, the rustbelt city of bridges, where I grew into myself *and* the spices of the popular *golden* milk. The cream cheese is laced with the orange and ginger notes of colorful turmeric with aromatic cardamom and cloves. It's a surprise flavor that will catch your friends off guard in the most pleasant way. To really embrace wintry January vibes (in honor of my birth month, obviously), serve with a warm, creamy golden milk latte.

Cheesecake Batter

16 oz (454 g) Neufchatel cheese or full-fat cream cheese, softened

1/2 cup (120 ml) honey

2 eggs

2 egg whites

2 tbsp (17 g) sorghum flour

3 tsp (15 g) ground turmeric

1 tsp (5 g) cinnamon

1/2 tsp ground ginger

1/2 tsp ground cardamom

1/4 tsp ground cloves

Brownie Batter

12 oz (340 g) dark chocolate chips

2 sticks unsalted butter

1 cup (192 g) coconut sugar or raw cane sugar

4 eggs

2 tbsp (30 ml) vanilla extract

1 cup (96 g) almond meal

1 cup (130 g) sorghum flour

1 tsp fine sea salt

1/2 tsp baking soda

To make the cheesecake batter, preheat the oven to 350°F (177°C) and line a 9 x 13–inch (23 x 33–cm) pan with parchment paper and spray well with cooking spray. In the bowl of a stand mixer, cream together the cream cheese and honey until smooth. Add the eggs and egg whites, and mix until incorporated. Stir in the flour, tumeric, cinnamon, ginger, cardamom and cloves, and mix until combined. Set the batter aside.

To make the brownie batter, using a double boiler/*bain marie* method, melt the chocolate and butter, stirring frequently until smooth. Remove from the heat, and allow to cool for a few minutes, then transfer to the bowl of a stand mixer. Whisk in the sugar. Add the eggs, one at a time, scraping down the bowl after each addition, then stir in the vanilla.

In a separate bowl, whisk together the almond meal, sorghum flour, salt and baking soda, then add to the chocolate mix in the stand mixer, and whisk until combined.

Reserve a 1/2 cup (123 g) of the brownie batter and set aside. Pour the rest of the brownie batter into the prepared pan, and smooth into a base layer.

Spread the cheesecake layer evenly on top of the brownie layer. Drop tablespoons of the reserved brownie batter on top of the cheesecake layer. Use a knife, chopstick or wooden skewer to swirl the batter.

Bake for about 30 to 35 minutes, until the top is set. Allow to cool completely before cutting into bars. Store in an airtight container, and keep refrigerated.

Just a *Little* Something Sweet: Dark Chocolate Truffles

QUINOA AND TEFF | MAKES 15–18 TRUFFLES

Dark chocolate truffles are perfect little night caps—a sweet note to end the day. This version mixes protein-rich quinoa with roasted almond butter, so there's a bit of a crunch beneath the dark chocolate and tart dried strawberry powder.

Of course, you can enjoy these truffles any time of year, but they're especially perfect for bypassing the commercial cards and cliché bouquets typically exchanged when Cupid calls. They're a chance to give a homemade token to the one you love, whether it be your life partner, a new significant other, a best friend or a close family member. These truffles are sweet, salty, tart little indulgences with the added benefit of quinoa.

¼ cup (43 g) uncooked quinoa

½ cup (120 ml) water

1 tsp coconut oil

¾ cup (135 g) unsalted roasted almond butter

3 tbsp (45 ml) honey

1 tbsp (15 ml) vanilla extract

1 tbsp (8 g) teff flour

1 tbsp (12 g) raw cacao powder

1½ tsp (4 g) cardamom

1 tsp sea salt

3.5 oz (100 g) 72% or higher dark chocolate (I used an 85% bar)

Freeze dried strawberries, for garnishing

Pink Himalayan sea salt, for garnishing

TIPS & TRICKS
Serve these suckers with champagne! It's a time to celebrate (even if it's just a Wednesday evening)!

Preheat the oven to 350°F (177°C). Line a baking sheet with parchment paper and set aside.

Pour the quinoa into a fine mesh strainer, and rinse for 2 minutes with cool water, swishing and mixing with your hand to rinse thoroughly. Drain. Heat a saucepan over medium-high heat. Add the drained quinoa, and toast until any remaining water has evaporated, 1 to 2 minutes. Add the water, and bring the quinoa and water to a boil, then cover, reduce the heat and simmer for 15 minutes. After 15 minutes, remove from the heat, and let stand, covered, for 5 minutes. Uncover, fluff with a fork, then stir in the coconut oil.

Spread the quinoa mixture into an even layer on the prepared baking sheet, and bake for 20 to 25 minutes, stirring twice for even toasting, until the quinoa turns golden brown and is crunchy. After baking, set aside to cool, then transfer to a mixing bowl.

In a food processor, combine the almond butter, honey, vanilla extract, teff flour, raw cacao powder, cardamom and sea salt until a soft "dough" forms. Transfer the mix to the bowl of toasted quinoa, and stir to combine.

Once combined, form into small, truffle size balls, about 15 total, and place on a baking sheet lined with parchment paper. Place in the freezer for 10 to 15 minutes to harden.

After the almond butter balls have chilled, melt the dark chocolate using a double boiler/*bain marie* method. Dip each ball in the chocolate and roll until fully coated, or use a spoon to drizzle with chocolate, then return to the parchment paper–lined sheet pan.

Use a mortar and pestle to crush a couple freeze-dried strawberries, then transfer the strawberry powder to a fine mesh strainer or a tea ball. Sprinkle the truffles with Pink Himalayan sea salt, then dust with the strawberry powder. Place in the fridge for 10 to 15 minutes or until they harden. Keep chilled until ready to serve.

Roasted Carrot Cheesecake with Ginger-Oat Crust

ROLLED OATS | MAKES 1 (9–INCH [24–CM]) CHEESECAKE

When nature packs so much sweetness and color in her produce, I can't help but turn it into sweets. Roasting carrots brings out even more of their natural sweetness, but unlike the ever popular carrot cake, this cheesecake lets the carrot's orange hue really shine against a sweet, spiced oat crust.

Roasted Carrots

2–3 tbsp (30–45 ml) coconut oil, melted
2 lbs (908 g) carrots, peeled (save the peels)

Crust

Melted coconut oil, for greasing
1½ cups (121 g) gluten-free oats
16 dried plums
1-inch (2.5-cm) chunk of fresh ginger, peeled
1 tsp ground cinnamon
½ tsp ground nutmeg
½ tsp ground cardamom
1 stick unsalted butter, melted

Filling

16 oz (454 g) cream cheese, softened
1 cup (145 g) light brown sugar
3 eggs, at room temperature
1 tsp vanilla extract
2 tsp (10 g) ground ginger
1 tsp cinnamon
½ tsp ground nutmeg
½ tsp ground cardamom

To Serve

Homemade whipped cream
Fresh mint leaves
Carrot peels
Maple roasted pecans

To make the carrots, preheat the oven to 400°F (204°C). Grease a sheetpan with 1 tablespoon (15 ml) of coconut oil. Arrange the carrots on the pan and brush with the remaining coconut oil. Bake for 20 to 25 minutes, until soft. Once cooled, purée them in a food processor or blender until creamy, and set aside. You should have about 1¾ cups (314 g) of the purée. Reduce the oven temperature to 350°F (177°C).

To make the crust, grease a 9-inch (23-cm) springform pan. Combine all of the crust ingredients in a food processor, and pulse until combined and paste-like. Press the mixture onto the bottom of the springform pan. Bake the crust for 10 minutes. Set aside to cool completely. Reduce the oven temperature to 275°F (140°C).

To make the filling, make sure your filling ingredients are at room temperature. In the bowl of a stand mixer, beat the cream cheese and brown sugar on medium speed until smooth. Add the eggs, one at a time, and mix for about 2 minutes total. Pour in the roasted carrot purée, vanilla, ginger, cinnamon, nutmeg and cardamom. Blend for another 2 minutes on medium speed, until well combined. Pour the filling over the cooled crust. Tap the pan on a counter a few times to release all of the air in the batter.

Place a shallow pan full of water on the lower rack in the oven. Position the cheesecake on the center rack. Bake for 60 to 70 minutes, or until the edge of the cheesecake is puffed and firm but the center is still wobbly and wet looking.

Turn off the oven, and with the door slightly opened (you can use a wooden spoon to prop it open), leave the cheesecake in the oven to cool completely, for at least an hour. Remove from the oven and transfer to a cooling rack and gently loosen the edges with an offset spatula or knife. Cool completely, then chill in the refrigerator for at least 6 hours, ideally overnight.

To serve, top with homemade whipped cream, and decorate with fresh mint, carrot peels and pecans.

TIPS & TRICKS
You can decorate with the raw carrot peels, but if you want to make them a more appetizing garnish, candy them by submerging the peels in simmering simple syrup (sugar water) for 2 to 3 seconds, then lift, drain and roll into roses or other flourishes.

Derby Day Mint Julep Cake

My sisters grew up in Iowa, riding horses (or more accurately, getting back on horses—conquer those fears!), but I grew up in the suburbs. I lived vicariously through *Thoroughbred*, the pre-teen book series that followed Ashleigh and her horse, Wonder. I rooted for Wonder, from weak foal to (spoiler alert) Kentucky Derby champion and bonded with my dad watching the Triple Crown races in real life.

There was something so intense about watching a reigning champion try to defy history and sweep the crown. Plus, those racetrack festivities . . . ! Donning a ridiculous floral hat and sipping a mint julep at the races became a bucket list dream of mine. I haven't made the trip yet, but in the meantime, a girl can celebrate with cake, drinks and my dog, Julep (but no whiskey or chocolate for her—poor thing!).

This festive cake combines two layers of whole-grain mint chocolate cake with whiskey whipped cream and a mint infused maple syrup for drizzling over each slice. Depending on how heavy handed your drizzle is, you'll have enough extra syrup to make Mint Juleps too. Just use it as you would a simple syrup, then raise a Julep cup to childhood heroes and bucket list dreams—cheers!

Mint Syrup
½ cup (120 ml) water
½ cup (120 ml) maple syrup
1 cup (40 g) chopped mint

Mint Chocolate Cake
⅔ cup (156 ml) avocado oil
4 large eggs
1⅓ cups (315 ml) buttermilk
2 tsp (10 ml) vanilla extract
2 tsp (10 ml) peppermint extract
1 cup (192 g) coconut sugar or raw cane sugar
1 cup (152 g) brown rice flour
½ cup (65 g) sorghum flour
1 cup (180 g) raw cacao powder, or cocoa
2 tbsp (16 g) arrowroot starch/flour
2½ tsp (9 g) baking powder
2 tsp (7 g) ground psyllium husk powder
1 tsp salt

Whiskey Whipped Cream
½ cup (120 ml) heavy cream, chilled
¼ cup (31 g) mascarpone cheese, chilled
1 tbsp (15 ml) mint syrup
½ tbsp (8 ml) vanilla extract
1–2 tbsp (15–30 ml) gluten-free whiskey, to taste
½ cup (65 g) powdered sugar, sifted

To Serve
Fresh mint
Edible flowers

(continued)

Derby Day Mint Julep Cake (continued)

To make the mint syrup, bring the water and maple syrup to a boil over medium-high heat in a small saucepan, then reduce the heat and simmer 5 minutes, stirring to dissolve the syrup. Turn off the heat, add the chopped mint and let infuse and cool for at least 20 minutes—the longer the better. Strain the mint, and transfer the syrup to a sealed container in the fridge for up to one week.

To make the cake, preheat the oven to 350°F (177°C). Lightly grease two 8-inch (20-cm) round pans.

In the bowl of a stand mixer, beat the oil, eggs, buttermilk and extracts until thoroughly combined.

In a separate medium mixing bowl, whisk together the sugar, brown rice flour, sorghum, cacao, arrowroot, baking powder, ground psyllium husk and salt.

In three increments, add the dry ingredients to the egg mixture, beating for 1 minute and scraping the bottom and sides of the bowl after each addition. Then beat at medium-high speed for 2 minutes, to make a smooth batter. Pour the batter into the prepared pans. The batter will be more liquidy than a traditional cake batter.

Bake the cakes for 40 to 50 minutes, about 3 to 4 minutes past the point where a toothpick inserted into the center comes out clean. The cakes' internal temperature should be 210°F (98°C). Remove the cakes from the oven, and let them cool in the pan for 10 minutes. Remove the cakes from the pans to cool completely on a rack.

To make the whipped cream, beat the heavy cream, mascarpone cheese, mint syrup and vanilla extract in the bowl of a stand mixer until soft peaks form, about 6 to 7 minutes. Add the whiskey and beat until just blended. With the motor turned off, sift the powdered sugar over the bowl, then mix until the texture is thick and creamy. Keep chilled until ready to use.

To assemble, if the cake layers are uneven, use a bread knife to level the surfaces. Smooth a dollop of whipped cream on the serving plate and top with the base layer of cake (the whipped cream keeps the cake in position). Cover the cake generously with whipped topping. Use a lazy Susan and an offset spatula to smooth the whipped cream. Top with the second layer of cake. Frost the sides and top. Keep the cake chilled until 15 minutes before serving. Garnish with fresh mint and flowers. Serve each slice with a drizzle of mint syrup, and enjoy!

TIPS & TRICKS
My mom's trick for foolproof whipped cream is to chill both the mixing bowl and the whisk attachment to keep everything nice and cool. The research on whiskey and celiacs is divided, so the best bet is to play it safe and use a gluten-free whiskey such as Jameson or Wild Turkey. You can also find more comprehensive lists of gluten-free whiskeys online.

Apple Season Layer Cake

BROWN RICE FLOUR | MAKES 2 (8-INCH [20-CM]) CAKES OR 1 LAYER CAKE

Everyone thinks farmers sit back and relax during the cold East Coast winters, but the reality is my fella keeps busy with planning, tending to heartier winter crops and pruning. Organic apple trees require lots and lots of pruning, but all that work pays off come fall when we feast on the sweetest, crispest apples. This cake is a celebration of the long-awaited fall harvest, when our region produces more apples and zucchini than we can keep up with.

Naturally, my first response is to convert the harvest into something sweet: layers of cake with apple butter buttercream and a sweet and tart apple cider reduction. Made with fiber-rich brown rice flour, sweetened with honey and loaded with zucchini and apple chunks, this cake will indulge your sweet tooth in a more wholesome way.

Cake

3 cups (454 g) brown rice flour

1½ tsp (6 g) baking powder

½ tsp baking soda

2 tsp (5 g) ground cinnamon

½ tsp fresh grated nutmeg

¾ tsp sea salt

¼ tsp ground cardamom

4 large eggs

1 cup (220 g) packed light brown sugar

1 cup (240 ml) honey

1 cup (240 ml) melted coconut oil

Finely grated zest from 2 medium lemons

2 tbsp (30 ml) fresh lemon juice

2 tsp (10 ml) vanilla extract

2 cups (180 g) zucchini, coarsely grated

Apple Butter Buttercream

4 oz (114 g) cream cheese, at room temperature

2 tbsp (30 g) salted butter, at room temperature

¼ cup (45 g) apple butter

¼ cup (33 g) powdered sugar, sifted

Apple Cider Reduction

6 cups (1.4 L) apple cider

1 tsp whole cloves

6–7 star anise pods

Lemon peels from 1 lemon

Spiced Apple Rosettes

1 lb (454 g) apples (about 3 apples)

¼ cup (55 g) firmly packed light brown sugar

½ tsp cornstarch

¼ tsp ground cinnamon

Pinch of sea salt

1 tbsp (15 g) butter

(continued)

Apple Season Layer Cake (continued)

To make the cakes, preheat the oven to 350°F (177°C). Grease the bottom and sides of two 8-inch (20-cm) springform cake pans. Set aside. In a mixing bowl, whisk together the flour, baking powder, baking soda, cinnamon, nutmeg, salt and cardamom. Set aside.

In the bowl of a stand mixer, beat together the eggs, brown sugar, honey, coconut oil, lemon zest, lemon juice and vanilla extract. Fold the flour mixture into the wet ingredients, until combined. Stir in the grated zucchini.

Divide the batter between the two prepared cake pans. Bake for 40 to 45 minutes, or until a toothpick comes out clean when inserted in the center. Transfer to a cooling rack to cool slightly, about 5 to 10 minutes. Remove the cakes from the pans and cool completely.

To make the buttercream, beat the cream cheese, butter, apple butter and powdered sugar together until smooth. Keep chilled until ready to use.

To make the cider reduction, bring the apple cider, cloves, anise pods and lemon peel to a boil in a large saucepan, then simmer over medium heat. As the sauce begins to thicken, remove the spices and lemon peels. Continue to simmer until reduced to about ¾ cup (177 ml), and the sauce is the consistency of honey, 30 to 40 minutes. Set aside and let cool completely.

To make the apple rosettes, cut the apples into ½-inch (13-mm)-thick wedges. Toss together the apples, brown sugar, cornstarch, cinnamon and salt. Melt the butter in a large skillet over medium-high heat. Add the apple mixture, and sauté 5 to 6 minutes or until tender and golden. Cool completely, about 30 minutes.

To assemble, using a lazy Susan and a bread knife, cut each cake into two layers. Place the bottom layer of cake on a serving plate/platter. Frost the layer of cake with a generous dollop of buttercream and smooth into an even layer. Add the next layer and repeat until all of the layers are in place. Frost the sides lightly and chill to set. Arrange the sautéed apples over the frosted cake and drizzle with the cider reduction.

Everything Cookies

BUCKWHEAT GROATS, OAT FLOUR, ROLLED OATS | MAKES ABOUT 2 DOZEN COOKIES

Whenever my mom flattened brown paper grocery bags over the table, I knew it was going to be a day filled with cookies. Instead of wire racks, she'd spread the cookies over the brown paper to cool and absorb any grease, then she'd repurpose the pan for another batch, until our long, farmhouse table was *covered* in cookies. Admittedly, I wasn't much of a kitchen helper, so the flavors were usually a surprise. As a picky kid, there was nothing worse than snagging a freshly baked cookie, expecting a chocolate chip and then biting into a raisin . . . forget about it!

Decades later, when I worked at Allegro Hearth Bakery, a perk of the job was taking home a confection at the end of a shift. There were three staple cookies on the menu: oatmeal raisin, chocolate chip and the most tender peanut butter cookie, all of them nearly as big as my face. After a long baking shift, it was too hard to make a decision.

This "everything cookie" is my solution to my childhood petulance and my adult analysis paralysis. It's all three of the classic flavors in one cookie, with an added buckwheat crunch. Now you don't have to choose, *and* you can feel good about eating this cookie as it's lightly sweetened and high in fiber and protein.

1 cup (180 g) creamy peanut butter

½ cup (110 g) packed brown sugar

½ cup (120 ml) honey

2 large eggs

2¼ cups (177 g) rolled oats

1 cup (130 g) oat flour

1 tsp baking soda

½ tsp salt

¾ cup (135 g) chocolate chips

½ cup (76 g) golden raisins

3 tbsp (32 g) buckwheat groats

Preheat the oven to 350°F (177°C). Line two sheet pans with parchment paper.

In the bowl of a stand mixer, cream together the peanut butter and the brown sugar until fluffy. Beat in the honey, then the eggs.

In a separate mixing bowl, whisk together the oats, oat flour, baking soda and salt. Add the oat mixture to the peanut butter batter, and whisk until combined. Fold in the chocolate chips, golden raisins and buckwheat groats.

Drop by tablespoonfuls, 2 inches (5 cm) apart, onto the baking sheets and flatten slightly. Bake for 20 to 25 minutes. Transfer the cookies to a wire rack to cool. Store any uneaten cookies in an airtight container.

Frozen Peach Pie Bars with Graham Cracker Crust

BROWN RICE FLOUR, SORGHUM FLOUR | MAKES 1 (9 X 13–INCH [23 X 33–CM]) PAN

"We're having company over" were the four words I *loved* to hear as a kid. Those words meant good eats were in store. Mom was always changing up the menus, but one menu item I requested religiously was her frozen peach dessert! She put together some magical combination of peaches, cool whip and maybe whipped cream, to create an airy, ice-cream-like filling, then added more graham cracker crumbs for good measure.

The frozen peach dessert was a lesson in patience—attempt to eat it too quickly after removing it from the freezer, and the fork might stab the slice right off the plate. Proper patience equated to that desired creamy bite. My version honors my mom but skips the cool whip and starts with a whole-grain gluten-free graham cracker crust (see Tips & Tricks). As an added bonus, you can use the crust recipe to make graham crackers for all your summer s'more gatherings). Win win!

Graham Cracker Crust

1 cup (152 g) brown rice flour, sifted

1 cup (130 g) sorghum flour, sifted

¼ cup (48 g) coconut sugar

½ tsp salt

1 tsp cinnamon

1 tsp baking powder

1 large egg

¼ cup (60 ml) melted coconut oil, plus more for greasing pan

¼ cup (60 ml) honey

2–3 tbsp (30–45 ml) heavy cream or milk

Peach Filling

32 oz (907 g) frozen peach slices, thawed

1 tbsp (15 ml) vanilla extract

2 tbsp (30 ml) maple syrup

2 cups (480 ml) heavy cream

To make the graham cracker crust, combine the flours, sugar, salt, cinnamon and baking powder in a medium-size bowl.

In a separate bowl, whisk the egg with the oil, honey and heavy cream. Stir this egg mixture into the dry ingredients until you have a fairly stiff dough, adding more cream if necessary. Wrap the dough and chill it until firm, about 1 hour (or longer, if it's more convenient). At this point, you can use the dough as crust or as graham crackers. See Tips & Tricks for cracker instructions.

Preheat the oven to 300°F (150°C). Grease a 9 x 13–inch (23 x 33–cm) pan with the coconut oil. Knead the dough gently until it holds together. Use your hands to press the dough into an even layer on the pan. Bake for 20 to 25 minutes, until golden brown. Turn off the oven, and open the oven door wide for 5 minutes. After the majority of the oven's heat has dissipated, shut the oven door and let it cool down for 20 minutes with the crust inside; this will help the crust to crisp.

To make the peach filling, purée the peaches in a food processor until no chunks remain. Add the vanilla extract and maple syrup, and pulse to combine. In the chilled bowl of a stand mixer, beat the heavy cream on medium-high until stiff peaks form. Add the peach purée, and continue to blend until combined.

Pour the peach mixture over the prepared crust. Transfer to the freezer, and freeze for at least 2 hours. Thaw slightly before serving for the creamiest texture.

> TIPS & TRICKS
>
> *To use the dough for graham crackers, divide the dough in half, and working with one piece at a time, knead the dough gently until it holds together. Roll the dough out, about ⅛ inch (3 mm) thick, onto a piece of parchment paper.*
>
> *Transfer the rolled-out dough to a baking sheet, and cut into 3 x 2–inch (8 x 5–cm) rectangles, reworking any dough scraps. Repeat with the second piece of dough. Sprinkle the dough with cinnamon and sugar. Bake the sheets of dough for 15 to 20 minutes, until golden and crisp around the edges, rotating the pans halfway through. Remove the crackers from the oven, transfer them to a cooling rack, and cool completely. Store the crackers, well-wrapped, at room temperature for up to a week; freeze for longer storage.*

Red, White & Blue Rustic Millet Skillet Cake

MILLET | MAKES 1 (10-INCH [25-CM]) CAKE

"I knew you must be special," she said, "because he told me he had a new 'lady-friend.'" I beamed back at her, like an idiot, imagining the Rustbelt Farmer telling his mama about me. Then I gushed on and on about our first encounters, the butterflies, the impatience, the will in my heart for the universe to make our paths cross, because if there's anyone who understands how special a man he is, it's his mother.

We held hands for the first time as the sky erupted with fireworks—the 4th of July makes for a dramatic anniversary—so when Independence Day rolls around, there's always cause for thematic desserts and celebrating. Baking this almond-flavored cake directly in a skillet removes the fuss that can come with a more complicated pan. There's no fear of flipping or collapsing, and this berry laden dessert is already transportable.

You don't need to wait for a national holiday to enjoy this cake to the fullest. Serve a slice with a generous scoop of vanilla bean ice cream or whipped cream and extra fresh berries any ol' time, including breakfast because this is whole-grain eating at its best!

Melted butter or coconut oil, for greasing
½ cup (120 ml) milk or heavy cream
Finely grated zest and juice of 1 lemon
1 cup (130 g) millet flour
1 cup (96 g) almond flour/meal
1 cup (192 g) coconut sugar or raw cane sugar
1½ tsp (6 g) baking powder
½ tsp baking soda
½ tsp sea salt
¾ cup (177 ml) extra virgin olive oil, plus more for pan
3 large eggs, room temperature
1 tsp (5 ml) pure almond extract
2 cups (303 g) blueberries

To Serve
Confectioners' sugar, for dusting
Vanilla ice cream or whipped cream
Blueberries
Cherries, pitted and halved

Preheat the oven to 325°F (165°C). Grease a 10-inch (25-cm) cast-iron skillet with the melted butter and set aside.

Combine the milk and lemon juice in a bowl; let stand until thickened, about 5 minutes.

Sift the millet flour, almond flour, coconut sugar, baking powder, baking soda and salt into a mixing bowl, and whisk to combine.

In the bowl of a standing mixer, beat the milk mixture, olive oil, eggs and almond extract until combined. Pour the liquid mix over the dry mix. Stir to combine, then fold in the blueberries.

Pour the batter into the skillet. Bake until the cake is golden and a tester inserted in the center comes out clean, about 55 minutes. Let cool completely in the pan on a wire rack.

Dust with the confectioners' sugar, and serve with a scoop of ice cream and fresh berries.

Twin Bing Cherry–Chocolate Popsicles with Honey Buckwheat Crunch

BUCKWHEAT GROATS | MAKES 10 POPSICLES, DEPENDING ON YOUR MOLD

When I first learned the concept of "foreigner," I enthusiastically believed being born in Nebraska made me a foreigner, and in turn, made me different and unique. This notion may have been bolstered by my father's "import" hobby. Anytime family made the trip from the Midwest to Pennsylvania, my dad requested hefty rations of Dorothy Lynch salad dressing and his favorite confection: Palmer Candy Company's Twin Bing, a cherry nougat covered in a "hash" of roasted peanuts and chocolate.

By alternating layers of unsweetened, puréed dark cherries and homemade whipped cream, this popsicle is the healthified version of my dad's indulgence. Whole buckwheat groats, which contain high levels of zinc, copper and manganese, combine with salty peanuts for a modern take on the heavily sweetened nougat, and it's all sealed in a dark chocolate drizzle. This is a satisfyingly sweet treat for hot days with minimal sugar.

Cherry Popsicles

32 oz (907 g) frozen dark sweet cherries, thawed

1 tsp almond extract, optional

½ cup (120 ml) heavy cream

1 tbsp (15 ml) maple syrup

1 tsp vanilla extract

Buckwheat Crunch

¼ cup (43 g) buckwheat groats

¼ cup (40 g) chopped salted and roasted peanuts

1½ tsp (7 ml) honey

Chocolate Dip

⅓ cup (58 g) dark chocolate chips

1 tbsp (15 g) coconut oil

To make the popsicles, assemble your popsicle mold and set aside. Using a food processor or blender, purée the cherries and almond extract, if using. In the chilled bowl of a stand mixer, whip the heavy cream, maple syrup and the vanilla extract until stiff peaks form. Spoon the cherry purée into the bottom third of each popsicle mold, followed by a third of whipped cream, then top off the mold with the remaining cherry purée. Transfer to the freezer, and freeze completely.

To make the buckwheat crunch, line a sheet pan with parchment paper and set aside. Heat a large skillet or pan on medium-high heat until hot. Do not add oil or butter to the skillet. Add the buckwheat groats and chopped nuts in a single layer.

Stir the buckwheat groats and nuts constantly, and shake the pan periodically to keep everything moving. Toast the mixture for approximately 2 to 3 minutes, or until the groats are browned but not burned. Remove from the heat, and stir in the honey. Continue to stir, off the heat, for 1 minute, then transfer to an even layer on the sheet pan.

To make the chocolate drizzle, line a baking sheet with parchment paper. In a saucepan over medium-low heat, melt the dark chocolate and coconut oil, stirring constantly, until combined, about 5 to 10 minutes. Remove the popsicles from the molds, and place each popsicle on the baking sheet. Sprinkle the buckwheat crunch over the popsicles, then drizzle the chocolate over (it will freeze quickly and secure the buckwheat crunch in place). Serve immediately, or freeze until ready to enjoy.

Creamy Chocolate-Amaranth Cupcakes with Bourbon Whipped Crème Fraîche

AMARANTH | MAKES 18–24 CUPCAKES, DEPENDING ON MUFFIN TIN SIZE

I'm all about decadent layer cakes, but when it comes to ease *and* show, creating a cupcake board can be just as impressive and better yet, interactive. Dessert will come alive as friends and family choose their own adventures. The starting point is the flourless Creamy Chocolate-Amaranth Cupcake, made somewhat magically, by blending cooked amaranth with standard baking ingredients. They're a bit spongey, akin to a flourless chocolate cake. It's tough to wait, but these cupcakes taste best—extra creamy and fudgie—the day *after* baking.

Arranging the cupcakes and planning the toppings is *your* chance to be creative. As a starting point, whip up a batch of Bourbon Whipped Crème Fraîche. It's fluffy and creamy, like a frosting, but it's not laden with sugar, which means you can plan on decorating and *eating* two cupcakes!

Amaranth Cupcakes

1 cup (170 g) amaranth
3 cups (720 ml) water
½ cup (120 ml) melted butter
4 eggs, at room temperature
⅓ cup (80 g) sour cream or Greek yogurt
¼ cup (60 ml) melted coconut oil or olive oil
1 tsp vanilla extract
1 cup (192 g) coconut sugar
1 cup (111 g) raw cacao powder or cocoa
1½ tsp (6 g) baking powder
½ tsp baking soda
½ tsp salt

Bourbon Whipped Crème Fraîche

¾ cup (177 ml) heavy cream
¼ cup (60 g) crème fraîche
2 tsp (10 ml) gluten-free bourbon
Maple syrup, to taste, optional

To make the cupcakes, bring the amaranth and water to a boil in a pot. Cover, reduce the heat and simmer until most of the water is absorbed, about 20 minutes. Remove from the heat and set aside to cool. The amaranth should absorb any remaining liquid as it cools. If not, strain the excess.

Preheat the oven to 350°F (177°C). Grease and line a cupcake tin with cupcake liners. Set aside.

In a blender or food processor, combine the cooked amaranth and melted butter until creamy. Add the eggs, sour cream, melted coconut oil and vanilla extract, then blend until completely smooth, 30 to 60 seconds.

In a large mixing bowl, sift together the sugar, cacao, baking powder, baking soda and salt. Pour the amaranth mixture into the bowl with the dry ingredients, and stir together until well combined. Divide the batter between the cupcakes and bake for about 12 to 15 minutes, or until a toothpick comes out clean.

To make the Bourbon Whipped Crème Fraîche, beat the heavy cream, crème fraîche and the bourbon until soft peaks form. For a sweeter topping, add the maple syrup to taste. The Bourbon Whipped Crème Fraîche can be made 4 hours ahead of time. Just cover, chill and then rewhisk before serving.

SOME OTHER TOPPING IDEAS TO GET YOUR CUPCAKE BUFFET STARTED
+ *Assorted frostings or flavor-infused whipped creams*
+ *Dark chocolate ganache or chocolate sauce*
+ *Caramel sauce or dulce de leche*
+ *Melted peanut butter*
+ *Assorted nuts and toasted coconut flakes*
+ *Chocolate chips, grated chocolate or raw cacao nibs*
+ *Fresh berries, and if you're feeling extra fancy, chocolate covered strawberries*

Maple-Sweetened Pecan Pie Bars

Brown Rice Flour, Teff Flour | Makes 16 bars

There are great historical moments that mark our lives, freezing us in the moment of where we were, who was with us and how we felt. Working the early morning shift at Allegro Hearth Bakery became my lunar landing. That was the morning when I heard the words "chocolate" and "pecan" used to describe the *same* pie. How had I, an admitted chocoholic (exhibit A: A Chocoholic's Brunch Salad on page 66!), never thought to combine those flavors in one pie?

I took that lesson to heart, and chocolate and pecans have become one of my fall holiday baking traditions. The beauty of these bars is they have all the rewarding flavors of pie without all the fuss. There's no rolling pin, or stressing over cracking dough. There's just a rich, buttery, whole-grain crust with maple syrup, dark chocolate and toasted pecans. One bite might cause you to tune out where you are and who's around you because sometimes escaping into a dessert is better than freezing time.

Crust

¼ cup (30 g) pecans

Melted butter or coconut oil, for greasing

½ cup (65 g) teff flour

½ cup (76 g) brown rice flour

2 tbsp (16 g) ground golden flaxseeds

⅓ cup (63 g) coconut sugar

½ tsp salt

4 tbsp (60 g) unsalted butter, cut into cubes and chilled

2 tbsp (30 ml) gluten-free bourbon or water

Filling

¼ cup (60 ml) browned butter, kept hot (see Tips & Tricks)

2 oz (57 g) baking chocolate, chopped

⅓ cup (63 g) coconut sugar

1 cup (240 ml) pure maple syrup

2 tbsp (30 ml) bourbon

¼ tsp sea salt

3 large eggs

1½ cups (181 g) chopped pecans, toasted

1½–2 cups (181–241 g) pecan halves, varies by design

To toast the pecans, preheat the oven to 350°F (177°C). Spread the chopped pecans in a single layer on a rimmed baking sheet and toast, stirring once or twice, until lightly browned and aromatic, 8 to 10 minutes. Set aside

To make the crust, adjust the oven rack to lowest position and heat the oven to 350°F (177°C). Line an 8 x 8–inch (20 x 20–cm) baking pan with parchment paper and lightly grease with the melted butter.

Pulse the toasted pecans, teff flour, brown rice flour, ground golden flaxseeds, sugar and salt in a food processor until the mixture resembles coarse cornmeal, about 5 pulses. Sprinkle the butter and bourbon evenly over the mixture, and pulse until the mixture again resembles coarse cornmeal, about 8 pulses. If you don't want to use bourbon, you can use water. The liquid is necessary to prevent a grittier texture. Transfer the mixture to the prepared pan and press firmly into an even layer using your fingers or the bottom of measuring cup. Bake until the crust begins to brown, 20 to 24 minutes, rotating the pan halfway through baking.

To make the filling, pour the hot browned butter over the chopped chocolate in a heatproof bowl, whisking to melt the chocolate and combine. Let it cool slightly.

In the bowl of a stand mixer, combine the browned butter mixture, coconut sugar, maple syrup, bourbon and salt, and beat until well combined. Add the eggs and beat until smooth. Fold in the chopped, toasted pecans. Pour the mixture over the crust, and use a spatula to spread the topping evenly, then arrange the pecan halves in a design, or just sprinkle over the surface. Depending on your design, you won't need the full amount of pecan halves.

Bake for 23 to 25 minutes, until the bars are bubbling across the entire surface. Transfer the pan to a cooling rack. Let the bars cool completely in the pan on the rack, about 1½ hours, then use the parchment paper to lift the bars from the pan and transfer to a cutting board. Cut into 16 bars. The bars can be stored at room temperature for up to 5 days.

Cranberry Cheesecake with Wine-Poached Pears

There are times when baking is *functional*. These are the times for quick batches of brownies or our go-to chocolate chip cookies. Then, there are times when baking is *ceremonial*. Cheesecake is the latter. Whether it's waiting for the ingredients to soften, or avoiding the temptation to peek into a hot oven, cheesecake is a commitment to time and patience, but after all that work, it's also a dessert to *eat* slowly, and patiently. The perfect bite is one that balances crust, cheese filling and topping harmoniously. It is not a haphazard forkful.

This cheesecake is worthy of special holiday occasions and winter hibernation days. It's a spiced oat crust—a mix that fills your kitchen with that revered Christmas morning aroma—with a decadently tall layer of cranberry-studded cheesecake. Then, like a good holiday party, this cheesecake gets a little boozy with wine-poached pears.

Crust

1½ cups (121 g) gluten-free oats

16 dried plums

1-inch (3-cm) chunk of fresh ginger, peeled

1 tsp (3 g) ground cinnamon

½ tsp ground nutmeg

½ tsp ground cardamom

1 stick unsalted butter, melted

Cheesecake Filling

4 (8-oz [227-g] packages cream cheese, at room temperature

1 cup (192 g) coconut sugar or raw cane sugar

4 eggs, at room temperature

8 oz (227 g) whole cranberries

Wine-Poached Pears

1 cup (240 ml) water

½ cup (120 ml) dry red wine

½ cup (120 ml) honey

1 tbsp (15 ml) vanilla extract

2 cinnamon sticks, plus more to garnish

6 whole cloves

2 whole star anise, optional

Zest of 1 orange

1 tsp (5 g) ground cardamom

2 firm but ripe large Bosc pears, peeled, halved, cored

Fresh herbs, to garnish

Citrus, to garnish

To make the crust, preheat the oven to 350°F (177°C). Place one rack on the lower third, and another rack in the middle. Grease a 9-inch (23-cm) springform pan. Combine the oats, plums, ginger, cinnamon, nutmeg, cardamom and butter in a food processor, and pulse until combined and paste-like. Press the mixture into the bottom of the springform pan. Bake the crust for 10 minutes. Set aside to cool completely. Reduce the oven temperature to 325°F (165°C).

To make the filling, make sure all of your ingredients are at room temperature. In the bowl of a stand mixer, beat the cream cheese and sugar on medium speed. Add the eggs, 1 at a time, mixing on low speed, until just blended. Fold in the cranberries, then pour the batter over the crust.

Place a pan of water on the bottom oven rack to prevent a dry cheesecake. Place the cheesecake on the middle rack. Bake for 55 to 65 minutes or until the center is almost set—some wobble is okay—as long as the edges are firm. For the best outcome, don't peek in the oven until later in the baking. Transfer to a cooling rack and cool for 15 minutes. Run a knife around the rim of the pan to loosen the cake; cool completely before removing the rim, then refrigerate the cheesecake for at least 4 hours before serving, ideally overnight.

To make the pears, combine the water, wine, honey, vanilla extract, cinnamon sticks, whole cloves, star anise, orange zest and cardamom in a 3- or 4-quart (2.8- or 3.8-L) saucepan. Stir over medium heat until the honey dissolves. Add the pears. Reduce the heat to medium-low, and cover. Simmer until the pears are just tender when pierced, turning the pears halfway through cooking, about 15 minutes.

Using a slotted spoon, transfer the pears to a large bowl. Bring the liquid to a boil, until reduced to ¾ cup (177 ml), about 2 minutes. Cool the syrup, strain the spices but reserve the cinnamon sticks for a garnish. Then pour the syrup over the pears. Cover and refrigerate until cold, at least 8 hours or overnight.

To serve, top the chilled cheesecake with the wine-poached pears, and drizzle with the reserved wine sauce. Garnish with fresh herbs, citrus and cinnamon sticks.

P.S. (Pup Sweets): Peanut Butter Pupcakes

Oat Flour, Rolled Oats | Makes 12 pupcakes

I couldn't talk this much about sharing and not share with my best girl, my fur baby, my Julep. She showed me a simplicity to life—friendship and play—go a long way in bringing contentment to a day. Work hard, play hard and nap harder. She made me a better neighbor and taught me to expect the best from people. I've also watched her brighten the days of so many folks around us.

My deep love for my four-legged kitchen companion has had me researching all sorts of recipes and dog food schools of thought. There's no short answer when it comes to what's the *best* way to feed her, but I've seen how switching Julep's diet to homecooked meats, veggies and whole grains has improved her coat and kept her teeth looking pearly.

Whole-grain oats contain more fat and protein than most grains, so these pupcakes will help your fur baby maintain energy and in colder months, warmth. Oats improve the body's resistance to stress, so treat these pupcakes as a visual cue to slow down, take a walk, throw a ball and enjoy the furry one you love. Plus, you can eat these treats too!

1 large egg

1 banana

½ cup (45 g) finely grated carrots

⅓ cup (60 g) peanut butter

⅓ cup (78 ml) melted coconut oil

¼ cup (60 ml) honey

1 cup (130 g) oat flour

¼ tsp baking soda

⅓ cup (27 g) rolled oats

Preheat the oven to 350°F (177°C) and line a cupcake tin with paper liners.

In a blender or food processor, beat the egg, banana, carrots, peanut butter, coconut oil and honey until smooth.

In a separate bowl, sift the oat flour and baking soda together. Add the rolled oats and whisk to combine. Pour the liquid ingredients over the dry mixture, and stir to combine.

Scoop the batter into the prepared cupcake liners, about two-thirds full.

Bake for 15 to 20 minutes, until a toothpick inserted in the middle of a cupcake comes out clean.

Tips & Tricks
For a pup-friendly "frosting," add a dollop of creamy peanut butter or whip softened cream cheese and pumpkin purée together.

Acknowledgments

I'm big on thank yous, so here goes . . . !

To Kyle, from the outside, it seemed like you had the optimal gig—number one taste tester—but in reality, you had a front row seat to the chaos. This process was no cakewalk, but you shared it *all* with me, from celebratory champagne toasts at the beginning, to crunchtime stresses, fears, recipe fails and meltdowns. You were my number one supporter, and I couldn't have done this without you. I love you, and I'm immensely grateful for this life we share, and I do believe we are due for a vacation!

To Julep, my fur baby and guru. Whether recipes landed or whether they flopped, you were always there, quietly waiting to clean up the crumbs and kiss my face. You forced me to take breaks, breathe some fresh air and smile all the time. XOXO, mama

To Lindsey, oh friend, my best sharing friend, I can't thank you enough! In a cosmic sense, I know you had something to do with this book falling into place. In a very *real* sense, you had *everything* to do with this book moving forward. You gave me space when I needed to focus, an ear when I needed to vent (about rice, for way too long. I'm sorry!) You knew just when I needed dog GIFs to lift my spirits. I am so grateful to call you my friend. Now let's eat some doughnuts and make all of *our* ideas happen!

To Noah, thank you, thank you, thank you for investing your skills, talents and above all, your support and enthusiasm in this book and in me. You are a master of light and "excessive scrims" (joke's on everyone else!). You reminded me to be excited in spite of stress, helped me to find words when all I had was exhaustion (*can* you right click with your left hand?) and managed to turn off this brain of mine and remind me to breathe. Thank you to Sarah, too, for sharing you and for reporting back on all the recipes. Sarah, you're my favorite Granola Monster!

To my parents, Doug and Regina, you taught me to dream big, to be thoughtful, to think of others and that it's rude to eat in front of someone and not share. I am immensely grateful.

To my sisters, each of you shaped me in so many ways. To Stacy, you nurtured my love of words and language from such a young age, as well as encouraged dancing in anticipation of baked goods. To Tonya, thank you for always embracing me just as I am, for modeling independence and determination, and for encouraging me to listen to the deepest inclinations of my heart. To Tosha, you told me I'd never cook for myself, or be taller than you, and look how far I've come! Ha! But seriously, you've laced my life with so many fond memories and made me feel so special. I value your love of nostalgia. To Dana, my sister by choice. Thank you for always being there for me, for dog walks, for ugly cries, for sharing your deck with its glorious sunsets and firework displays, and for understanding when my pie payments were late. I love you all!

To the Pattisons, thank you for embracing me as one of your own from day one. Thank you for checking in, for encouraging me, for helping me make car decisions when I had no time to make car decisions, for keeping my spine healthy after hunching over mixing bowls, for just being the best! I love you!

To Sarah Monroe and the Page Street Team, thank you for stumbling upon my corner of the web and for giving me this opportunity. Sarah, you'll never know just how crazily I danced with joy when I read your first email. You enabled a longtime dream of mine to come true.

To the many others who shaped this path of mine, and to those of you who have supported my blogging journey. I hope you see yourselves reflected in these pages, and I hope we find a way to a shared table.

About the Author

Quelcy Kogel is a multi-passionate creative who works as a food and prop stylist, event designer, writer and dog cuddler. As a stylist, Quelcy has worked with brands like Brooklyn Brewery, GNC, Healthyish Foods, Honest Tea, The Food Mood Girl and ModCloth to bring their brand stories to life. Quelcy was a regular contributor to Design*Sponge, focusing on sustainability and interior design. She founded her site, WithTheGrains.com, as a way to document her own wanderings, farm-to-table adventures and seasonal recipes. Her work has been featured on Bon Appétit, BuzzFeed, HuffPost Taste, the Instagram blog and in *Sift* magazine. She lives in a prop-filled apartment in Pittsburgh, Pennsylvania, with her boyfriend, Kyle, and their beloved pup, Julep.

Index

C